D1333160

BRAZEN

REBEL LADIES WHO ROCKED THE WORLD

PÉNÉLOPE BAGIEU

EBURY
PRESS

For my amazing daughters.
—P. B.

CONTENTS

CONTENTS

CLÉMENTINE DELAIT

BEARDED LADY

1865 - 1939

CLÉMENTINE IS A VERY STURDY LITTLE GIRL.

THIS PROVES QUITE HANDY FOR HER PARENTS ON THEIR FARM IN THE VOSGES MOUNTAINS.

Where do you want this, Daddy?

IN HER TEEN YEARS, CLÉMENTINE DISCOVERS THERE IS SOMETHING... EXTRA SPECIAL ABOUT HER...

What? What? Do I have lipstick on my teeth?

...AND SHE STARTS SHAVING HER FACE.

SOON THEREAFTER, SHE FALLS HEAD OVER HEELS FOR JOSEPH THE BAKER.

Tee hee...

Just buy the baguette already!

THE FEELING IS MUTUAL.

Do you, Clémentine

YES.

THE CUSTOMERS ARE MOST INTRIGUED BY THE NEW BAKER LADY.

Can I get you anything else??

BUT JOSEPH SUFFERS FROM TERRIBLE RHEUMATISM, AND CLÉMENTINE CAN'T BEAR TO SEE HIM IN PAIN ANYMORE.

My poor honey bun!

AND SO THE COUPLE REINVENTS THEMSELVES...

...AS CONTRIBUTORS TO THE LOCAL NIGHTLIFE.

♪ Ta-daaa!

OLD CHUMS BAR
FOR SALE
SOLD

JOSEPH KEEPS THE BOOKS...

...WHILE HIS WIFE HANDLES THE BAR...

No more, René! You're drunk as a skunk!

...AND, ON OCCASION, SECURITY.

Hmpff! I warned you, René!

PEOPLE EVERYWHERE ARE FASCINATED BY CLÉMENTINE.

Another round?

ONE DAY, AS SHE STROLLS THROUGH A CARNIVAL...

ZOLT

...SOMEONE CALLS OUT TO CLÉMENTINE.

Hey!

Hello, gorgeous!

THIS ENCOUNTER WILL TURN HER LIFE UPSIDE DOWN.

FOR CLÉMENTINE THEN MAKES A DECISION...

...THAT TRANSFORMS HER DESTINY.

I will *never* shave again.

You likey?

BEARDED LADY'S CAFE

PEOPLE CROWD INTO THE PLACE TO BE SERVED BY THE VOSGES' OWN CELEBRITY.

Can I touch it?

What is *wrong* with you?

BUOYED BY HER METEORIC RISE TO FAME, CLÉMENTINE STARTS SELLING PHOTOS OF HERSELF. THEY'RE A HIT.

It's for Robert.

For Robert... Hugs and kisses...

SHE IS EVEN GRANTED PERMISSION TO DRESS AS A MAN FOR THESE PHOTOS (WHICH IS STRICTLY FORBIDDEN IN THESE DAYS).

Whatsa matter? Cat got your tongue?

CLÉMENTINE BECOMES A TRUE STAR, TWINKLING FAR BEYOND THE VOSGES.

Pardon me... Are you Clémentine Delait?

SHE IS THE MASCOT OF THE WWI SOLDIERS—AKA THE "HAIRY ONES."

I'll trade you this for "Clémentine at the beach," 'Kay?

BOOM!

THE DELAITS ADOPT A LITTLE WAR ORPHAN, FERNANDE.

Whoa, easy there, pumpkin!

A CARNIVAL DIRECTOR COMES TO SEE CLÉMENTINE ONE DAY, OFFERING HER VAST SUMS OF MONEY TO JOIN HIS SHOW.

You'll be the main attraction! You'll see the world!

What is *wrong* with you?

CLÉMENTINE RECEIVES INVITATIONS FROM ALL THE CROWNED HEADS OF EUROPE.

Look, Lizzie, you won't see that every day.

TRAGICALLY, JOSEPH IS SNATCHED AWAY FROM HER A SHORT WHILE LATER.

Farewell, honey bun.

NOW A RICH AND FAMOUS WIDOW, SHE WONDERS WHAT TO DO WITH HER LIFE.

JOIN A CIRCUS?

TRAVEL AROUND THE WORLD?

After all, I'm only sixty-three. I've got my whole life ahead of me.

SHE DECIDES TO GO BACK TO HER ROOTS, RETURNING HOME TO THE VOSGES TO OPEN A NEW CAFÉ.

René!

AND SO CLÉMENTINE LIVES OUT HER DAYS PEACEFULLY BEHIND A BAR IN THAON-LES-VOSGES...

Well...

not exactly "behind..."

...WHERE SHE, FERNANDE, AND A PET PARROT PERFORM CABARET ACTS.

IN THE END, A HEART ATTACK TAKES HER LIFE. SHE LEAVES BEHIND AN EPITAPH SHE CHOSE HERSELF.

Here lies Clémentine Delait, the Bearded Lady

NZINGA

QUEEN OF NDONGO AND MATAMBA

1583-1663

KING KILUANJI FATHERS FOUR CHILDREN, WHOM HE LOVES TENDERLY.

BUT HIS FAVORITE BABY IS BORN IN 1583,

WITH THE UMBILICAL CORD WRAPPED AROUND HER NECK.

THE WORD "KUJINGA" ("TO TWIST OR TURN" IN KIMBUNDU) GIVES THE LITTLE GIRL HER NAME.

Nzinga.

THE MIDWIFE MAKES THIS PROPHECY.

She will be my queen.

FROM THEN ON, NZINGA RULES THE HEART OF HER SMITTEN FATHER, WHO TAKES HER EVERYWHERE HE GOES.

EVEN TO WAR, WHICH IS RAGING BETWEEN NDONGO (PRESENT-DAY ANGOLA) AND PORTUGUESE INVADERS LAUNCHING REPEATED ATTACKS.

WHEN THEIR FATHER DIES, HER BROTHER MBANDI, THOUGH HARDLY THE BRIGHTEST BULB, ASCENDS THE THRONE.

HE IS WARY OF NZINGA, AND FOR GOOD REASON— SHE IS MUCH SMARTER THAN HIM.

OUT OF SUSPICION AND PARANOIA, HE EVEN DECIDES TO HAVE HIS SISTER'S SON KILLED, JUST TO BE SAFE...

...THEREBY TURNING HER INTO HIS SWORN ENEMY NUMBER ONE.

THE NEW KING ISN'T SURE WHAT TO DO WITH THIS QUICK-WITTED YOUNG WOMAN AND HER FINELY TUNED MIND.

Let me handle the politics so I don't get in your way.

Your Majesty.

Yes, good idea. I am a very busy king. Go negotiate with the Portuguese. Ask them to leave while you're at it (heh heh heh).

NZINGA IS SIXTEEN WHEN THEY SEND HER TO TALK WITH THE PORTUGUESE.

Seriously?

THEY FIGURE IT WILL BE SINFULLY EASY TO DEAL WITH AN IMPRESSIONABLE KID.

And this, little girl, is a *"pistol."*

IN ORDER TO EMBARRASS AND RATTLE HER, THE GOVERNOR DOESN'T OFFER HER A SEAT.

Har Har Har

a mat on the ground, traditionally reserved for inferiors in Mbundu culture

BUT NZINGA REFUSES TO BE HUMILIATED IN SUCH A WAY.

Okay then.

Let's begin.

IT IS THUS AS AN EQUAL THAT NZINGA, A FORMIDABLE NEGOTIATOR, SPELLS OUT HER CONDITIONS.

You are going to withdraw from Ambaca and free the slaves.

THE PORTUGUESE SIGN THE TREATY...

...BUT NEVER HONOR IT.

IN 1641, THE DUTCH SEIZE LUANDA.

Pssst!

NZINGA OFFERS THEM AN ALLIANCE AGAINST THE PORTUGUESE TRAITORS.

DURING THIS TIME, NZINGA'S FAMILY SUFFERS A STRANGE RUN OF FATAL TRAGEDIES.

HER BROTHER MBANDI IS THOUGHT TO HAVE BEEN POISONED.

Nah. He *killed* himself.

MBANDI'S SON ALSO DIES PREMATURELY.

Well *him*, yeah, sure.

I had him taken out.

FROM THEN ON, NZINGA COMMANDS HER PEOPLE TO CALL HER THE *QUEEN OF NDONGO*.

WHILE SHE'S AT IT, SHE HAS HERSELF OFFICIALLY PROCLAIMED A "MAN," AND DECREES THAT SHE WILL NEVER TAKE A KING.

(BUT SHE HAS COUNTLESS LOVERS.)

NZINGA SPENDS MOST OF HER ENERGY ON HER FAVORITE PASTIME.

Whacking the Portuguese!!!

SHE LEADS HER ARMIES INTO BATTLE WELL INTO HER LATER YEARS.

DESPITE MANY ATTEMPTS TO OVERTHROW HER (WHICH SHE FOILS EACH AND EVERY TIME), AND DESPITE THE OPPRESSION FROM THE EUROPEAN POWERS (WHICH SHE SUCCESSFULLY TURNS AGAINST ONE ANOTHER)...

NZINGA OF NDONGO HOLDS THE POWER SHE SEIZED BY FORCE FOR NEARLY FORTY YEARS.

SHE DIES AT THE AGE OF EIGHTY, AFTER FINALLY BROKERING A PEACE DEAL WITH THE PORTUGUESE.

statue in Luanda, Angola

MARGARET HAMILTON
TERRIFYING ACTRESS

1902 – 1985

(NOT TO BE CONFUSED WITH HER EQUALLY COOL NAMESAKE WHO DESIGNED THE ONBOARD SYSTEM FOR THE APOLLO PROGRAM)

← Margaret with her stacks of source codes for Apollo 11

NO, OUR MARGARET IS BORN IN CLEVELAND IN 1902, AND DOES NOT DREAM OF SPACE EXPLORATION.

Oh no!

(THOUGH SHE WILL END UP FLYING IN THE SKY.)

I want to be an *actress!*

AUDITION

...

Next!

MARGARET DREAMS OF ROMANTIC ROLES.

And here's one last piece of advice...

...get a nose job!

NATURALLY, MARGARET DOES NOT SHARE THAT OPINION.

My nose is just fine!

That guy's crazy.

SHE DECIDES TO CHANGE HER STRATEGY.

Are you here for the role of the beautiful, fragile fugitive, too?

Would you mind if I auditioned for the part of the mean and ugly stepsister instead?

IN ADDITION TO HER NEW M.O., MARGARET USES AN APPROACH GUARANTEED TO LAND HER AS MANY GIGS AS POSSIBLE.

I'm the cheapest in town!

TO MAKE DO AS A SINGLE MOM, SHE TAKES ON ALL THE MEAN ROLES, INCLUDING THE PART OF A WITCH IN A MUSICAL.

Mwa ha ha

WHEN SHE LEARNS THE PLAY WILL BE ADAPTED FOR THE BIG SCREEN...

This is my big *chance*!

...SHE SHOWS UP AT THE AUDITION FULLY DETERMINED TO LAND THE PART.

Show time, Maggie.

AFTER AUDITIONING, MARGARET IS STILL SO MUCH IN CHARACTER THAT SHE BURSTS OUT INTO A DEMONIC LAUGH THAT SCARES THE CASTING DIRECTORS TO DEATH.

MWA HA HA HA

Th... thanks.

THE GORGEOUS ACTRESS THE PRODUCERS INITIALLY HAVE IN MIND REFUSES TO BE MADE UGLY FOR THE FILM (EVEN TO PLAY A WITCH) AND SO MARGARET IS OFFERED THE PART, ALONGSIDE HOLLYWOOD A-LISTERS.

FILMING ON *THE WIZARD OF OZ* BEGINS IN 1938. MARGARET IS MADE TO LOOK THE PART.

Your nose and your chin are too small. We're going to stick fake ones on.

I must be dreaming, ha ha!

AS A FINAL TOUCH, HER SKIN IS COVERED IN A THICK LAYER OF GREEN MAKEUP.

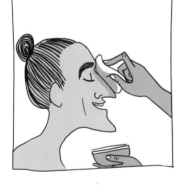

THE EFFECT IS STRIKING.

THE FILM IS A MAJOR FEAT OF TECHNOLOGY FOR ITS DAY.

Toto, help!

IN THE FIRST SCENE AFTER DOROTHY LANDS, THE WITCH IS SUPPOSED TO VANISH FROM THE TERRIFIED MUNCHKINS IN A BIG CLOUD OF SMOKE AND FIRE.

MWA HA HA HA

TRAGICALLY, AN ACCIDENT OCCURS, AND THE FLAMES ARE SET OFF BEFORE MARGARET HAS TIME TO HIDE UNDER THE STAGE.

HER BROOM, HER FACE, AND HER HANDS CATCH ON FIRE.

HER THICK, COPPER-BASED GREEN MAKEUP HAS TO BE VIGOROUSLY RUBBED OFF HER CHARRED SKIN WITH ALCOHOL. THE PAIN IS UNIMAGINABLE.

Hold her down.

IT TAKES MARGARET THREE MONTHS TO RECUPERATE...

Get well soon, Judy

...BUT SHE MAKES HER WAY BACK TO THE STUDIO TO FINISH THE FILM.

THE SKIN ON HER HANDS ISN'T EVEN COMPLETELY HEALED YET.

SHE HAS TO WEAR GLOVES FOR THE REST OF THE SHOOT.

THE FILM FINALLY WRAPS. MARGARET'S SKIN REMAINS GREEN FOR WEEKS TO COME.

Aaaaaa

Are you sure you're okay?

You look a little sickly.

MGM ORGANIZES A TEST SCREENING FOR CHILDREN.

THE VERDICT IS INCONTROVERTIBLE: THE WITCH IS WAY TOO SCARY. HALF OF MARGARET'S SCENES ARE CUT.

After all I went through!

AFTER *THE WIZARD OF OZ*, MARGARET JACKS UP HER RATES SIGNIFICANTLY.

FOLLOWING HER UNFORGETTABLE PERFORMANCE, SHE IS, PERHAPS NOT SURPRISINGLY, TYPECAST IN THE ROLES OF CANTANKEROUS WITCHES.

Morticia's mother in the TV series *The Addams Family*

BUT THIS DOESN'T BOTHER MARGARET, WHO IS FULLY AWARE OF HER UNIQUE GIFT.

WHEN IT COMES TO BEING SCARY, SHE IS THE BEST.

SHE APPEARS IN AN EPISODE OF *SESAME STREET*.

AN EPISODE THE NETWORK TAKES OFF THE AIR FOR GOOD AFTER PARENTS COMPLAIN.

THE WICKED WITCH OF THE WEST IS RANKED FOURTH GREATEST VILLAIN IN THE MOVIES BY THE AMERICAN FILM INSTITUTE AFTER...

- HANNIBAL LECTER

- NORMAN BATES

And me

THE WIZARD OF OZ IS THE MOST WATCHED FILM IN THE WORLD. (IT EVEN MADE THE UNESCO WORLD HERITAGE LIST.) MARGARET HAMILTON TRAUMATIZES GENERATIONS OF CHILDREN WITH THE ROLE THAT GOT UNDER HER SKIN AND STAYED THERE UNTIL SHE DIED.

Boo.

THAT'S SOME IRONIC TWIST OF FATE FOR A MILD-MANNERED WOMAN WHO STARTED OUT AS A SCHOOLTEACHER.

The end!

LAS MARIPOSAS

REBEL SISTERS

THE MIRABALS HAVE FOUR DAUGHTERS. THEY LIVE IN OJO DE AGUA, IN THE DOMINICAN REPUBLIC.

Patria
Adela
Minerva
María Teresa

BY A STROKE OF LUCK, ALL FOUR OF THEM ARE BRILLIANT, DETERMINED, AND BEAUTIFUL.

AT THIS TIME, THEIR COUNTRY IS RUN BY A HORRIBLE DICTATOR WHO CALLS HIMSELF "EL JEFE" (THE BOSS).

Rafael *Trujillo*

TRUJILLO HAS BEEN IN POWER SINCE 1930. A CRUEL DESPOT, HE KEEPS TABS ON THE OPPOSITION THANKS TO A MUCH-FEARED SECRET POLICE. NASTY BUSINESS.

VIVA EL JEFE

THE LITTLE MIRABAL GIRLS GROW UP CAREFREE IN A WELL-TO-DO FAMILY. THEY ATTEND A CATHOLIC SCHOOL.

AT FIFTEEN, MINERVA ANNOUNCES SHE WANTS TO GO TO COLLEGE.

Er... okay.

AROUND THIS TIME, SHE BEGINS LISTENING TO FOREIGN RADIO BROADCASTS AND QUESTIONING HER COUNTRY'S POLITICS.

Huh? What? A *"tyrant"*?

SHE DECIDES TO STUDY LAW IN COLLEGE.

Here, read this.

MARX

SHE MAKES COMMUNIST FRIENDS THERE.

SHE MEETS A YOUNG IDEALIST NAMED PERICLES FRANCO,

THE FUTURE FOUNDER OF THE POPULAR SOCIALIST PARTY. HIS VIEWS HAVE ALREADY LANDED HIM IN PRISON. HE AWAKENS MINERVA'S ANTI-ESTABLISHMENT SPIRIT.

BUT AN UNEXPECTED EVENT WILL PRECIPITATE THE POLITICAL ACTIVISM OF THE MIRABAL SISTERS.

JUST LIKE A MODERN AND RATHER DISMAL CINDERELLA BALL, THE GIRLS ARE INVITED TO ONE OF THE BIG RECEPTIONS AT TRUJILLO'S PALACE.

IT IS EL JEFE'S HABIT TO PICK PRETTY YOUNG WOMEN AND PARADE THEM AROUND ON HIS ARM.

HE IMMEDIATELY SETS HIS SIGHTS ON MINERVA (WHOSE REACTION IS RATHER LUKEWARM).

LATER THAT SUMMER, HE INVITES HER TO ANOTHER SOIREE. SHE ATTENDS IT WITH HER SISTERS. HE RENEWS HIS ADVANCES.

Would you like to see my plane?

I'm good, thanks.

What a loser.

HE THEN INVITES HER TO HIS BEACH HOUSE. ONE OF HIS HENCHMEN DELIVERS THE MESSAGE.

No pressure.

THE MIRABALS ARE SERIOUSLY CONCERNED FOR MINERVA.

You should probably go...

...but we're coming with!

AS USUAL, THE DICTATOR IS QUITE PERSISTENT.

So, gorgeous, you like big guns?

BUT MINERVA HAS HAD ENOUGH.

WILL YOU PLEASE JUST LAY OFF?!!!

HER PARENTS PICK THIS MOMENT TO VAMOOSE.

AND WHILE WE'RE AT IT: LEAVE MY FRIEND PERICLES ALONE!!!

Thanks, great party.

PATRIA AND MARÍA TERESA, WHO SHARE THEIR SISTER'S REBELLIOUS SPIRIT, COULDN'T BE MORE PROUD OF HER.

I mean really!

ALAS, THE HUMILIATION IS NOT WITHOUT CONSEQUENCES, AND A FEW DAYS LATER, THEIR FATHER IS LOCKED UP.

Daddy!!

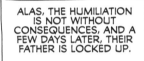

MINERVA AND HER FRIENDS ARE NEXT ON THE LIST.

FOR WEEKS, THEY'RE INTERROGATED ABOUT THEIR ASSOCIATION WITH THE POPULAR SOCIALIST PARTY...

...AND ABOUT MINERVA'S RELATIONSHIP WITH PERICLES.

Seriously?

MINERVA IS OFFERED FREEDOM IN EXCHANGE FOR A LETTER OF APOLOGY TO TRUJILLO.

Okay then.

p-tchoo!

SHE IS EVENTUALLY RELEASED. SHE GOES BACK TO SCHOOL, WHERE SHE MEETS HER FUTURE HUSBAND, MANOLO.

Long live the bride! And the Revolution!

(MANOLO, NATURALLY, IS FERVENTLY ANTI-TRUJILLO HIMSELF).

TWO OF HER SISTERS ALSO MARRY FIERCE OPPONENTS OF EL JEFE.

THE MIRABAL FAMILY SOON BOASTS A WHOLE FLOCK OF LITTLE REVOLUTIONARIES.

Down with tyranny!

Mooooommy!

MINERVA WRITES HER THESIS ON HUMAN RIGHTS AND, MOST IMPORTANTLY...

...the need for a regime change!

IN 1957, SHE BECOMES HER COUNTRY'S FIRST FEMALE DOCTORAL CANDIDATE IN LAW.

EL JEFE HIMSELF HANDS HER THE DIPLOMA.

Congrats.

HE MAKES HER A PROMISE RIGHT THEN AND THERE.

You'll never practice law.

I'll see to it personally.

RIGHT ABOUT NOW, LATIN AMERICAN DICTATORS ARE STARTING TO BE OVERTHROWN. THE REVOLUTION IN CUBA GIVES HOPE TO THOSE SUFFERING UNDER TRUJILLO.

CUBA HELPS THEM ATTEMPT A COUP AGAINST EL JEFE ON JUNE 14. IT FAILS, BUT INSPIRES THE NAME OF A GROUP OF DISSIDENTS. (MINERVA ATTENDS THEIR FIRST SECRET MEETING.)

Manolo, cofounder and president of the 14th of June Movement.

THE THREE MIRABAL SISTERS GO BY A CODE NAME. THEY CALL THEMSELVES THE SPANISH WORD FOR "BUTTERFLIES"...

LAS MARIPOSAS.

14TH OF JUNE MEMBERS ARE ARRESTED ON A REGULAR BASIS,

ESPECIALLY LAS MARIPOSAS AND THEIR HUSBANDS.

THEY ARE LOCKED UP AND TORTURED IN THE NOTORIOUS LA CUARENTA PRISON.

AS THEIR POPULARITY CONTINUES TO GROW, THEY RECEIVE SUPPORT FROM THE CATHOLIC CHURCH AND INTERNATIONAL PUBLIC OPINION.

THEY ARE RELEASED AFTER SERVING FIVE YEARS FOR "THREATENING NATIONAL SECURITY." THEIR HUSBANDS REMAIN IN PRISON.

IN THE EYES OF THE DOMINICAN PEOPLE, THEY ARE THE FACE OF THE REVOLUTION...

...AND BECOME AN EVEN GREATER CONCERN TO TRUJILLO, WHO CAN FEEL THE WINDS OF CHANGE COMING.

LAS MARIPOSAS ARE ON EDGE. THEY WORRY ABOUT THOSE FAMOUS "CAR ACCIDENTS" THAT HAPPEN SO OFTEN THESE DAYS.

THEY ARE RIGHT TO WORRY: ON NOVEMBER 25, 1960, WHILE DRIVING TO THE PRISON TO VISIT THEIR HUSBANDS, A CAR CUTS THEM OFF. THEY ARE HACKED TO DEATH WITH A MACHETE, THEN THEIR BODIES ARE PUT BACK INTO THE JEEP, WHICH IS HURLED OVER A CLIFF.

BUT THE PEOPLE DON'T BUY IT. THEY KNOW EXACTLY WHO WAS BEHIND IT ALL: THE INCREASINGLY UNPOPULAR DICTATOR, WHO THEN ANNOUNCES:

The only way I'm leaving is on a stretcher!

HE, TOO, TURNS OUT TO BE CLAIRVOYANT, FOR ON MAY 30, 1961, HIS OWN CAR IS IN AN "ACCIDENT," RIDDLED WITH SOME SIXTY BULLETS. HIS ASSASSINS GO ON TO BECOME NATIONAL HEROES.

TODAY, LAS MARIPOSAS' HOME REGION HAS BEEN RENAMED "HERMANAS MIRABAL."

AND THE INTERNATIONAL DAY FOR THE ELIMINATION OF VIOLENCE AGAINST WOMEN TAKES PLACE EACH YEAR ON NOVEMBER 25.

JOSEPHINA VAN GORKUM

OBSTINATE LOVER

1820 – 1888

JOSEPHINA IS BORN ON JUNE 28, 1820 IN ROERMOND, IN THE SOUTHERN NETHERLANDS.

HER FULL NAME IS:

Josephina
Caroline
Petronella
Hubertine
Van Aefferden

LET'S CALL HER JOSEPHINA.

SHE IS THE NEXT TO LAST OF HER FAMILY'S TEN CHILDREN, BORN TO TWO CATHOLIC ARISTOCRATS.

Her mother, Maria Agnes, most certainly has nannies.

SHE DISCOVERS HER LOVE OF FREEDOM AT AN EARLY AGE.

ONE DAY, JOSEPHINA MEETS JACOB. IT IS LOVE AT FIRST SIGHT.

THERE'S NOTHING ABOUT JACOB WERNER VAN GORKUM THAT HER FAMILY APPROVES OF.

First he's ten years older than you!

ALSO, HE'S A MILITARY MAN, WHICH IS **NOT** APPROPRIATE FOR A **JONKVROUW** (A YOUNG WOMAN OF GOOD BREEDING).

That... that uniform is very becoming.

41

BUT WORST OF ALL, JACOB IS A PROTESTANT.

(THE LOVERS COULDN'T CARE LESS AND GET MARRIED IN 1842.)

INDEED, THIS DIFFERENCE OF RELIGION, BEYOND SHOCKING THE NOTABLES OF ROERMOND, PRESENTS A REAL PROBLEM. IN THESE DAYS, DUTCH SOCIETY IS BUILT ON A DELIBERATE FORM OF SEGREGATION:

PILLARISATION

IT IS ALL ABOUT DISTINGUISHING THE "PILLARS" OF SOCIETY (CATHOLICS, PROTESTANTS, JEWS), WHO KEEP TO THEIR OWN WORLDS AND HAVE THEIR OWN SYSTEMS, AND, MOSTLY, MARRY WITHIN THEIR GROUPS.

IN SHORT, JOSEPHINA AND JACOB'S UNION FUELS THE RUMOR MILL.

Good! Keeps them busy!

THE YOUNG COUPLE ARE VERY MUCH IN LOVE, AND PILLARISATION DOESN'T STOP THEM FROM HAVING THREE CHILDREN.

JOSEPHINA GRADUALLY FINDS A WAY TO MAKE HER ATYPICAL FAMILY MODEL WORK IN SUCH A RIGID SOCIETY.

NEVERTHELESS, THERE IS ONE INJUSTICE THE VAN GORKUMS CAN'T ESCAPE:

I'll tell you one thing, lady, you won't be...

...buried together!

42

RIGHT AROUND THIS TIME, JOSEPHINA BECOMES FED UP WITH PILLARISATION.

Okay. Thank you.

UNDER THE LAW, SHE IS INDEED TO BE BURIED IN THE VAN AEFFERDEN FAMILY VAULT...

...AND HER HUSBAND AT THE OTHER END OF THE CEMETERY.

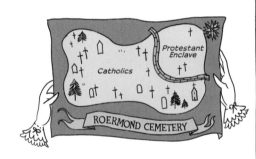

Protestant Enclave

Catholics

ROERMOND CEMETERY

SHE, OF COURSE, DOESN'T SEE IT THAT WAY.

Don't worry, dear, I'll find a solution.

JACOB DIES IN 1880. JOSEPHINA JOINS HIM ON NOVEMBER 29, 1888.

FOLLOWING JOSEPHINA VAN GORKUM'S WISHES, THE ROERMOND CEMETERY, TO THIS DAY, FEATURES...

...AN UNUSUAL GRAVESTONE ON EITHER SIDE OF THE WALL THAT RUNS THROUGH IT.

LOZEN
WARRIOR AND SHAMAN

~1840 - 1889(?)

LOZEN IS BORN NEAR THE SACRED MOUNTAIN OF OJO CALIENTE, IN A CHIRICAHUA VILLAGE AROUND 1840. HER BROTHER VICTORIO WILL LATER BECOME A GREAT APACHE WARRIOR AND CHIEF.

LOZEN PROVES TO BE COLORFUL EARLY ON: SHE IS BORED BY THE CHORES RESERVED FOR APACHE WOMEN.

BANG!

SHE WANTS IN ON THE *ACTION*.

SHE PARTICIPATES IN THE RITE OF PASSAGE CEREMONY, HER FIRST STEP INTO WOMANHOOD...

...BUT AFTERWARD SHE ANNOUNCES SHE WILL NEVER MARRY.

I'd rather devote myself to my people.

If that's cool with you.

THE CHIRICAHUAS, AT THE TIME, DO REALLY NEED HER HELP.

Let's go.

IN THESE DAYS, HER TRIBE'S TERRITORY STRADDLES THE ARIZONA AND NEW MEXICO BORDER.

"Apache-land"

SAN CARLOS, THE RESERVATION HER FAMILY IS STUCK IN, IS KNOWN FOR BEING ONE OF THE WORST. THE LIVING CONDITIONS ARE HORRIFIC.

VICTORIO BECOMES THE TRIBAL CHIEF AND TAKES HIS MEN TO ATTACK THE COLONIES IN NEW MEXICO.

I'm warning you: my sis is coming with.

Got it?

SHE'S NOT JUST HIS "RIGHT-HAND MAN." VICTORIO DESCRIBES HIS SISTER AS "STRONG AS A MAN AND BRAVER THAN MOST OF THEM."

(Not to mention a skilled horse thief.)

WHEN LOZEN WAS A CHILD, SHE WENT TO THE SACRED MOUNTAINS TO PRAY. SINCE THAT DAY, SHE HAS BEEN ENDOWED WITH STRONG SHAMANIC POWERS, WHICH PROVE HANDY ON THE BATTLEFIELD.

SHE CAN RUN AS FAST AS A HORSE AND HEAL WOUNDS. IN ADDITION, THIS WARRIOR CAN FEEL IN THE PALM OF HER HAND THE POSITION AND NUMBERS OF HER ENEMIES, THANKS TO THE HELP OF USSEN, THE APACHE SUPREME DEITY.

ANOTHER WOMAN FIGHTS ALONGSIDE LOZEN: DAHTESTE.

AN EXPERIENCED SCOUT WHO SPEAKS SEVERAL LANGUAGES, SHE'S THE APACHES' MESSENGER AND MEDIATOR.

49

LOZEN IS MUCH MORE THAN A FEMALE WARRIOR: SHE'S THE PROTECTOR OF HER TRIBE, LEADING THE WOMEN AND CHILDREN DOWN THE PERILOUS PATH OF EXODUS.

Follow me! Don't be afraid!

Take care of them. I'm heading back to the battlefield.

IN 1880, THE MEXICANS ATTACK THE APACHE HIDEOUT OF TRES CASTILLOS. BUT LOZEN HAS TO DEAL WITH SOMETHING UNEXPECTED.

What? Now?!!

WITH ONLY A HORSE AND A LOADED GUN, SHE SETS OFF WITH THE YOUNG MOTHER AND HER NEWBORN. SAFETY IS A THREE-DAY RIDE AWAY.

USING HER KNIFE TO HUNT WITHOUT ATTRACTING THE UNWANTED ATTENTION THAT GUNSHOTS BRING...

...AND SOMETIMES CROSSING PATHS WITH AMERICAN AND MEXICAN SOLDIERS...

...WHO SHE NEVER NEGLECTS TO RELIEVE OF THEIR HORSES, WEAPONS, AND SUPPLIES...

And often their shirts.

...LOZEN MANAGES TO ESCORT MOTHER AND CHILD TO SAFETY.

Okay, back at it!

BUT WHILE SHE'S GONE, HER BROTHER AND HIS MEN ARE AMBUSHED AND TAKEN CAPTIVE.

LOZEN HEARS THE NEWS AND RUSHES OFF TO FREE HIM AND THE PRISONERS.

ALAS, SHE ARRIVES TOO LATE. IT IS SAID THAT VICTORIO OPTED TO KILL HIMSELF RATHER THAN GIVE IN TO HIS CAPTORS.

BLINDED BY RAGE AND GRIEF, LOZEN ATTACKS THE MEXICANS RELENTLESSLY FOR TWO MONTHS BEFORE JOINING FORCES WITH GERONIMO.

SHE FIGHTS AT HIS SIDE UNTIL HIS SURRENDER IN 1886.

What... what the hell are you doing?!!

I'm tired, Lozen.

SHE IS IMPRISONED FAR FROM HOME IN THE SWAMPLAND OF ALABAMA. DISEASE RAVAGES THE BARRACKS WHERE SHE IS HELD.

LOZEN NEVER RETURNS TO HER HOMELAND. LIKE MANY APACHE PRISONERS, SHE SUCCUMBS TO TUBERCULOSIS AND IS BURIED IN AN UNMARKED GRAVE.

Piñedopez

ANNETTE KELLERMAN

MERMAID

1886 - 1975

AN AUSTRALIAN VIOLIN-PLAYING DADDY AND A FRENCH PIANO-PLAYING MOMMY WELCOME LITTLE ANNETTE TO THE WORLD ON JULY 6, 1886.

BUT THE POOR CHILD CONTRACTS POLIO AT THE AGE OF SIX.

SHE IS WEIGHED DOWN BY CONTRAPTIONS FOR YEARS. A DOCTOR SUGGESTS THAT HER PARENTS TAKE HER SWIMMING TO STIMULATE HER MUSCLES.

Are you sure, Doc?

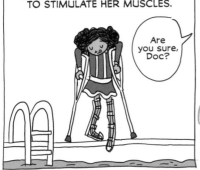

SO ANNETTE STARTS SWIMMING.

ALL THE TIME.

BY AGE FIFTEEN HER LEGS ARE HEALED...

...AND SHE HAS SET RECORDS IN THE 100 YARDS AND THE MILE FREESTYLE COMPETITIONS.

THE YOUNG GIRL TAKES A LIKING TO COMPETITION AND DECIDES TO CHALLENGE ATHLETES FROM EUROPE.

Let's do this!

AUS

SHE ATTEMPTS TO SWIM ACROSS THE ENGLISH CHANNEL THREE TIMES (IN VAIN).

(BUT SHE BEATS ALL HER MALE COMPETITION.)

THE EUROPEANS ARE VERY INTRIGUED BY THE NINETEEN-YEAR-OLD LITTLE AUSTRALIAN GIRL SWIMMING IN THE SEINE.

Bonjour!

ANNETTE DISCOVERS A LIKING (AND A REAL TALENT) FOR STAGING ATHLETIC PERFORMANCES.

COME AND MEET THE FISH LADY!

SHE FOCUSES INCREASINGLY ON THE ENTERTAINMENT ASPECT OF HER SPORT AND PUTS ON SENSATIONAL SHOWS.

dizzying dives

shows in aquariums

costumes

AT THIS TIME, WOMEN'S SWIMSUITS ARE CUMBERSOME, HEAVY, AND UNCOMFORTABLE GETUPS.

At least we won't get tan lines.

EVEN IN AUSTRALIA, VICTORIAN RIGIDITY PROHIBITS WOMEN FROM SWIMMING IN BROAD DAYLIGHT UNTIL 1903.

Close your eyes, Junior! There's an indecent woman showing her ankles!

Where? Where?

ANNETTE IS ONE TO KNOW: SWIMSUITS ARE DESIGNED FOR EVERYTHING...

...EXCEPT SWIMMING.

SO SHE STARTS TO CONCEIVE OF AN OUTFIT THAT WILL GIVE WOMEN FREEDOM OF MOVEMENT IN THE WATER.

straps

close to body

legs unfettered

SHE DESIGNS A PROTOTYPE AS BEST SHE CAN BY SEWING UNDERGARMENTS TOGETHER...

...AND THEN DEBUTS IT DURING AN INVITATION TO SWIM FOR THE ROYAL FAMILY IN LONDON.

TA-DAAAA!

THE AUDIENCE IS OUTRAGED, BUT ANNETTE, WITHOUT KNOWING IT, IS ABOUT TO TURN WOMEN'S LIVES UPSIDE DOWN.

SHE TAKES HER DISCOVERY ONE STEP FURTHER AND CUTS OFF THE LEGS ON HER SUIT.

Oh yeah! ♡

ANNETTE'S IMMODESTY IS TOO MUCH FOR THE AMERICAN POLICE, WHO ARREST HER ON A MASSACHUSETTS BEACH IN 1907.

You should be ashamed, young lady!

SHE ARGUES THAT HER SUIT IS A "TECHNICAL NECESSITY" LINKED TO HER SPORT.

Acquitted.

THIS RUN-IN WITH THE LAW BRINGS INTERNATIONAL FAME TO HER SWIMSUIT: THE "KELLERMAN" IS PROMPTLY ADOPTED BY PINUP MODELS FOR BEACH SHOOTS...

...WHICH INSPIRES ANNETTE TO MAKE IT AVAILABLE TO ALL WOMEN.

Last one in the water's a rotten hag!

EVEN HOLLYWOOD STARTS TO TAKE AN INTEREST IN THE MERMAID PROVOCATEUR.

Rolling...

SHE'S A NATURAL. WHO ELSE COULD ACT, DESIGN HER OWN COSTUMES, AND DO HER OWN STUNTS?

You think swimming with gators is doable?

Totally.

A NEW CINEMATIC GENRE IS BORN WITH HER MOVIES, MARKING THE BEGINNING OF SYNCHRONIZED SWIMMING. ANNETTE PAVES THE WAY FOR ACTRESSES LIKE ESTHER WILLIAMS...

(who will later play Annette on the big screen in 1952).

AT THE PINNACLE OF HER CAREER AS AN AQUATIC ACTRESS, SHE MARRIES HER MANAGER.

A HARVARD PROFESSOR STUDIES HER PROPORTIONS, WHICH HE LIKENS TO THOSE OF THE VENUS DE MILO, AND PRONOUNCES ANNETTE THE "PERFECT WOMAN."

Yeah, right.

Except for the brain!

SAYS THE SUBJECT, WHO DOESN'T REALLY CARE.

THE ONLY FILM OF HERS STILL AROUND TODAY IS *VENUS OF THE SOUTH SEAS*...

ANNETTE ACTUALLY PERFORMS IN SOME TWENTY FILMS. THE MOST FAMOUS AMONG THEM REMAINS *DAUGHTER OF THE GODS*—IT IS THE FIRST FILM TO COST MORE THAN ONE MILLION DOLLARS TO MAKE.

BUT WHAT STRIKES PEOPLE MOST WHEN THE FILM COMES OUT IS ANNETTE'S PERFORMANCE IN THE MAIN ROLE...

...BUCK NAKED.

(ANOTHER BIG FIRST FOR MOVIEMAKING AT THE TIME.)

Since apparently I have a perfect body, why hide it?

CONSTANTLY ASKED THE SECRET BEHIND HER GREAT PHYSICAL FORM, ANNETTE DECIDES TO PUBLISH HER ADVICE.

Annette Kellerman
HOW TO SWIM

HER BOOK'S SUCCESS INSPIRES HER TO OFFER MAIL-ORDER BOOKLETS.

Be *Beautiful* and *Healthy*

With Annette Kellerman!

WELL-BEING AND FITNESS GRADUALLY BECOME ANNETTE'S FAVORITE INTERESTS.

SHE TOUTS THE ADVANTAGES OF PHYSICAL FITNESS TO WOMEN, WHO IN THESE DAYS ARE NOT USED TO SUCH DISCOURSE.

CONVINCED THAT HEALTH STARTS WITH NUTRITION, SHE ALSO OPENS UP A VEGETARIAN GROCERY STORE IN CALIFORNIA.

THE AUSTRALIAN MERMAID PENS A CHILDREN'S BOOK ABOUT THE LEGENDS OF THE SOUTHERN SEAS.

SHE CONTINUES TO SWIM EVERY DAY FOR THE REST OF HER LIFE...

...(EVEN AT AGE EIGHTY-NINE)...

...AND AT LAST HER ASHES ARE SCATTERED OVER THE GREAT BARRIER REEF.

ATHLETE? ACTRESS? BUSINESSWOMAN? IT'S HARD TO PIN DOWN ANNETTE KELLERMAN'S LEGACY...

...THOUGH A GOOD WAY TO SUM UP HER LIFE COULD BE:

I helped to free women's bodies.

DELIA AKELEY
EXPLORER

1875-1970

DELIA IS THE LAST OF NINE CHILDREN BORN TO PATRICK AND MARGARET DENNING, EXTREMELY POOR IRISH IMMIGRANTS FROM BEAVER DAM, WISCONSIN.

SHE'S A QUIET, RESERVED CHILD WHO DOES HER HOUSEHOLD CHORES WITHOUT COMPLAINING.

HER FATHER IS PRONE TO ANGER. ONE DAY, WHEN SHE IS THIRTEEN, HE BAWLS HER OUT ONE TOO MANY TIMES.

AND SO DELIA LEAVES HOME

FOR GOOD.

SHE FLEES TO CHICAGO...

...WHERE SHE BECOMES THE ASSISTANT OF PROMINENT TAXIDERMIST CARL E. AKELEY.

Your... your eyes, sir.

Thank you, my dear.

AKELEY IS A CELEBRITY AMONG NATURALISTS. HE CREATES THE FAMOUS DIORAMAS AT THE AMERICAN MUSEUM OF NATURAL HISTORY.

THEY MARRY IN 1902.

SHE ACCOMPANIES HIM ON HIS TRAVELS TO AFRICA, WHERE HE HUNTS FOR SPECIMENS WITH GREAT FANFARE.

DELIA LEARNS HOW TO MANAGE ALL THE EXPEDITION DETAILS IN THE FIELD.

Not now, please! He's napping.

WHILE HUNTING IN KENYA, CARL IS ATTACKED BY AN ELEPHANT.

HIS ENTIRE TEAM HIGHTAILS IT OUT OF THERE, LEAVING HIM FOR DEAD, ALONE WITH HIS WIFE...

...WHO CARRIES HIM OVER THE MOUNTAINS TO THE NEAREST HOSPITAL.

SHE SAVES HIS LIFE MORE THAN ONCE THROUGHOUT HIS CAREER.

I... I see my mommy...

THEY BRING A LITTLE MONKEY BACK FROM ONE OF THEIR EXPEDITIONS, WHOM DELIA NAMES J.T. JR.

HE KEEPS HER COMPANY DURING THE ENDLESS EVENINGS CARL SPENDS WITH HIS CO-EDS.

EVENTUALLY, THE AKELEYS GET DIVORCED.

CARL PROMPTLY REMARRIES.

HIS NEW WIFE, NEARLY TWENTY-FIVE YEARS HIS JUNIOR, IS NOW THE ONE WHO ACCOMPANIES HIM ON HIS EXPEDITIONS, BUT SHE ISN'T ABLE TO SAVE HIM FROM EBOLA TWO YEARS LATER.

DELIA FINDS HERSELF AT LOOSE ENDS.

SHE'S FIFTY YEARS OLD.

SO SHE DECIDES TO EMBARK ON HER FIRST SOLO AFRICAN EXPEDITION.

I mean, I know what I'm doing, after all this time.

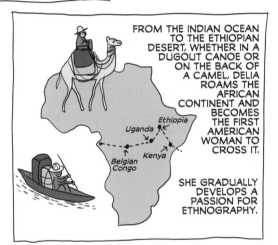

FROM THE INDIAN OCEAN TO THE ETHIOPIAN DESERT, WHETHER IN A DUGOUT CANOE OR ON THE BACK OF A CAMEL, DELIA ROAMS THE AFRICAN CONTINENT AND BECOMES THE FIRST AMERICAN WOMAN TO CROSS IT.

SHE GRADUALLY DEVELOPS A PASSION FOR ETHNOGRAPHY.

Uganda
Ethiopia
Belgian Congo
Kenya

SHE DEVOTES THE FOLLOWING YEARS TO EXPANDING HER RESEARCH BY MEETING WITH THE MYSTERIOUS PYGMY PEOPLES SHE FINDS SO FASCINATING.

She lives among them for several months in the Ituri forest.

←

SHE PUBLISHES HER NOTES, PRIMARILY THE ONES ON PRIMATOLOGY.

J. T. JR
Biography of an African Monkey
Delia Akeley

DELIA AKELEY PASSES AWAY IN FLORIDA AT THE AGE OF ONE HUNDRED.

NOW THAT'S WHAT YOU CALL A GREAT SECOND ACT IN LIFE.

JOSEPHINE BAKER

DANCER, FRENCH RESISTANCE FIGHTER, MATRIARCH

1906-1975

CARRIE AND EDDIE HAVE A LITTLE CABARET ACT IN THE STREETS OF SAINT LOUIS. (ALSO, THEY'RE IN LOVE.)

IN 1906, THEY HAVE A DAUGHTER: FREDA JOSEPHINE.

SHORTLY AFTER HER BIRTH, SHE HITS THE STAGE.

BUT A FEW MONTHS LATER, EDDIE BOWS OUT AND CARRIE IS LEFT TO FEND FOR HERSELF.

JOSEPHINE QUICKLY FOLLOWS IN HER PARENTS' FOOTSTEPS.

TO HELP PROVIDE FOR HER FAMILY, WHICH EXPANDS WITH EACH OF HER MOTHER'S LOVE AFFAIRS, THE LITTLE GIRL CLEANS THE HOUSES OF WEALTHY WOMEN (WHO ARE PRONE TO MISTREATING HER FROM TIME TO TIME).

SHE MARRIES A BOY NAMED WILLIE AT THE AGE OF THIRTEEN.

ONE YEAR LATER, SHE BREAKS A BOTTLE OVER HIS HEAD. (UNSURPRISINGLY, THEY GET A DIVORCE.)

SHE DECIDES TO GO WITH HER GUT AND TRIES TO JOIN A PROFESSIONAL DANCE TROUPE.

SHE'S HIRED FOR SHOWS THAT FEATURE BLACK DANCERS ONLY.

SHE EVENTUALLY PERFORMS ON BROADWAY, WHERE SHE'S NOTICED CLOWNING AROUND IN CHORUS LINES.

BUT SHE HAS CAUGHT THE RIGHT PERSON'S ATTENTION.

I'm looking for black artists for a show I'm doing in Paris.

JOSEPHINE HESITATES...FOR ABOUT THREE SECONDS...

...BEFORE DITCHING HER MOM (WITH WHOM SHE HAS AN ABYSMAL RELATIONSHIP), POVERTY, AND AMERICA.

So long!

SHE LANDS IN CHERBOURG IN 1925.

LA REVUE NÈGRE PREMIERES AT THE CHAMPS-ELYSÉES THEATER. THE PARISIANS ARE BLOWN AWAY BY THIS NEW SONG CALLED "THE CHARLESTON."

FRANCE IS DISCOVERING A BLACK CULTURE THAT IS A FAR CRY FROM ITS COLONIAL CLICHES; BUT MOSTLY, IT IS DISCOVERING *JOSEPHINE*.

WHO BECOMES AN OVERNIGHT SENSATION AMONG THE CUBISTS.

Josephine, by Calder, 1928

THIS METEORITIC RISE TO FAME INSPIRES HER TO SPREAD HER WINGS: SHE LEAVES *LA REVUE NÈGRE* AND BECOMES THE LEAD ACT AT THE FAMED FOLIES BERGÈRE.

THIS IS WHERE SHE CREATES HER FAMOUS "DANSE SAUVAGE" (THE GREAT-GRANDMOTHER OF THE TWERK).

SHE FALLS HEAD OVER HEELS FOR A BROODING, EGOCENTRIC PART-TIME GIGOLO FROM SICILY NAMED GIUSEPPE "PEPITO" ABATINO.

HE BECOMES HER MANAGER.

FOR TEN YEARS, HE STAYS AT JOSEPHINE'S SIDE THROUGH THICK AND THIN.

Break a leg!

SHE CREATES A NEW ACT, IN WHICH SHE SHARES THE SPOTLIGHT WITH A CHEETAH NAMED CHIQUITA.

Chiquita is a prankster and often escapes from the stage.

ON TOUR, CHIQUITA SLEEPS IN HIS MISTRESS'S BED, NOT HIS. IN PARIS, HE SHARES THE DRESSING ROOM WITH THE REST OF JOSEPHINE'S MENAGERIE.

Toutoute

Albert

SHE TRIES HER LUCK IN THE MOVIES AND PLAYS ALONGSIDE JEAN GABIN (WITH A SCREENPLAY BY PEPITO).

first major role in the movies for a black woman

THE RECEPTION IS MIXED. JOSEPHINE HAS THE BRIGHT IDEA TO START A SINGING CAREER.

J'ai deux amooours! *

* *"I have two loves"*

THIS TIME, THE AUDIENCE IS ON BOARD IMMEDIATELY.

JOSEPHINE HAS NO INTENTION OF BEING A FLASH IN THE PAN. BEING THE HARD WORKER SHE IS, SHE PUTS HERSELF ON A STRICT REGIMEN TO IMPROVE HER VOICE (WHICH SHE DOES). IN 1934, OFFENBACH'S OPERETTA *LA CRÉOLE* IS ADAPTED FOR HER AT THE MARIGNY THEATER.

SHE PERFORMS IN FRENCH, SHE SINGS IN FRENCH, AND SHE LOVES PARIS... JOSEPHINE HAS COME A LONG WAY FROM *LA REVUE NÈGRE*— SHE DOESN'T CARE TO BE SOME EXOTIC ODDITY ANYMORE.

I was suffocating in the States. Paris liberated me!

OF COURSE, HER ADOPTED COUNTRY HAS NEITHER RACIAL SEGREGATION (SHE CAN GO WHEREVER SHE PLEASES), NOR PURITANICAL MORALS.

(JOSEPHINE HAS SLIGHTLY MORE THAN "TWO LOVES.")

AROUND THIS TIME, SHE ATTEMPTS A NEW YORK COMEBACK (IN THE *ZIEGFIELD FOLLIES*). BUT JOSEPHINE IS A LITTLE UNDERDRESSED FOR THE U.S., WHICH SNUBS HER.

It's their loss!

Enough is enough! I'm going back to France *for good*.

JOSEPHINE BAKER IS FINALLY GIVEN OFFICIAL CITIZENSHIP IN HER BELOVED ADOPTED COUNTRY...

...JUST IN TIME TO WITNESS THE NAZI OCCUPATION.

Oh no you *don't*! I went through so much trouble to become French!

There must be *something* I can do...

AND THIS IS HOW JOSEPHINE BECOMES A SPY FOR THE FRENCH RESISTANCE.

using her life as a socialite to steal top secret information

This is utterly ridiculous!

Zimple ferification, fraulein!

sending messages in invisible ink on her sheet music

AFTER LIBERATION, IN APPRECIATION OF THE RISKS SHE TOOK, SHE IS AWARDED JUST ABOUT EVERY MILITARY HONOR AVAILABLE.

sub-lieutenant of the Women's Auxiliary of the French Air Force

SHE GETS MARRIED (YET AGAIN).

Jo Bouillon, Conductor

Fifth time's the charm!

TRAGICALLY, SHE HAS A VIOLENT MISCARRIAGE. THE TREATMENT LEAVES HER UNABLE TO EVER HAVE CHILDREN.

SHE DECIDES TO BUY A BIG CHATEAU AND ADOPTS A SLEW OF KIDS FROM ALL OVER THE WORLD (HER "RAINBOW TRIBE").

SHE PERFORMS ALL OVER THE PLACE, INCLUDING IN THE U.S., WHERE RACIAL SEGREGATION CONTINUES ITS COURSE.

WHITE WOMEN ONLY

SHE GETS INTO TIFFS WITH CLUB OWNERS, CAUSES SCANDALS IN BARS, AND REFUSES TO ACCEPT MONEY FROM SEGREGATED VENUES.

Grace Kelly

Let's go, Jojo!

Why you dirty...

SHE UNDERSTANDS THE ROAD THAT LIES AHEAD AND MARCHES ALONGSIDE MARTIN LUTHER KING, JR.

WE MARCH FOR

FROM THEN ON, SHE DEVOTES ALL HER ENERGY TO CIVIL RIGHTS AND THE FIGHT AGAINST RACIAL DISCRIMINATION.

Look at this march. Salt and pepper— just like it should be.

THE NATIONAL ASSOCIATION FOR THE ADVANCEMENT OF COLORED PEOPLE (NAACP) PRESENTS HER WITH A LIFETIME MEMBERSHIP AND DECLARES MAY 20 JOSEPHINE BAKER DAY.

JOSEPHINE ISN'T PERFORMIMG AS MUCH AND HER FINANCIAL SITUATION BECOMES SOMEWHAT ERRATIC.

Yay, Mommy!!

Noodles!!

HER HEART SINKS WHEN SHE IS EXPELLED FROM HER ESTATE ALONG WITH HER (MANY) CHILDREN.

SOLD

BUT JOSEPHINE CAN COUNT ON HER FRIEND GRACE KELLY, NOW PRINCESS OF MONACO, WHO OFFERS HER AN APARTMENT...

Don't you worry, dear Jojo.

...AND WITH THE HELP OF ANOTHER FRIEND, JACKIE KENNEDY ONASSIS, FINANCES HER RETURN TO THE STAGE.

Josephine à Bobino, 1975

IN THE MIDDLE OF HER PARIS TOUR, ON APRIL 12, 1975, JOSEPHINE HAS A STROKE AND DIES. THE BOBINO THEATER PAYS FOR THE FUNERAL EXPENSES.

A cheap casket won't do for Josephine!

THOUSANDS OF FANS CROWD INTO THE FUNERAL SERVICE. IN ACCORDANCE WITH HER WISHES, THE FLOWERS, SENT FROM ALL OVER THE WORLD, ARE LAID ON THE TOMB OF THE UNKNOWN SOLDIER.

Farewell, Zouzou

SHE IS BURIED IN THE MONACO CEMETERY, AFTER RECEIVING FULL FRENCH MILITARY HONORS (DURING WHICH HER SONG "J'AI DEUX AMOURS" IS PLAYED).

IN ADDITION TO HER "TRIBE" (TWELVE KIDS, IN ALL), SHE LEAVES BEHIND A NONPROFIT THAT PURSUES HER WORK ON BEHALF OF ABANDONED CHILDREN.

WHILE OFTEN REDUCED TO A BANANA BELT, JOSEPHINE BAKER WAS AN INCREDIBLY ENGAGED, ALTRUISTIC, AND COURAGEOUS WOMAN.

THIS KID FROM MISSOURI HAS A CRATER ON VENUS NAMED AFTER HER— NOTHING LESS WOULD DO.

TOVE JANSSON
PAINTER, CREATOR OF TROLLS

1914 - 2001

TOVE MARIKA JANSSON IS CONCEIVED IN PARIS AND BORN IN HELSINKI ON AUGUST 9, 1914.

SHE STARTS DRAWING BEFORE SHE CAN EVEN WALK.

HER FATHER, VIKTOR, IS A SCULPTOR, AND THE FAMILY LIVES IN AN ARTIST STUDIO.

TOVE GROWS UP IN A JOYOUS, CREATIVE HOUSEHOLD, WHERE PARENTS AND CHILDREN PAINT, TELL STORIES, AND HAVE PARTIES FOR DAYS ON END.

HER MOTHER, SIGNE, IS AN ILLUSTRATOR. SHE DRAWS, RIDES HORSES, SHOOTS RIFLES, AND KEEPS HER HUSBAND AND THREE CHILDREN FED. SHE IS A ROLE MODEL FOR HER DAUGHTER.

SHE ENCOURAGES HER LITTLE GIRL TO DO WHAT SHE LOVES AND NOT TO WORRY ABOUT WHAT OTHERS EXPECT OF HER.

TOVE PUBLISHES HER FIRST BOOK AT THE AGE OF THIRTEEN.

SHE STUDIES ART IN STOCKHOLM, ROME, AND PARIS.

84

BUT TOVE HAS A HARD TIME FINDING HER PLACE IN INSTITUTIONS, WHERE IT IS MADE CLEAR TO HER THAT WOMEN AREN'T WELCOME.

Art must come from the **balls**, you see?!

...

MOST OF HER CLASSMATES QUIT THEIR STUDIES IN ART TO DEVOTE THEMSELVES TO THEIR FAMILIES.

Well, personally, I just don't have **the time** to get married! Or to admire and comfort my man! I would be either a bad wife or a bad painter!

SHE DITCHES SCHOOL AND FOUNDS A COLLECTIVE OF ARTISTS

(AND GOES BACK TO HELSINKI).

UPON HER RETURN TO FINLAND, WORLD WAR II BREAKS OUT.

HER YOUNGER BROTHER GOES OFF TO FIGHT.

HER BEST FRIEND, A JEW, FLEES TO AMERICA. TOVE IS TRAUMATIZED BY THE WAR.

SHE FUNNELS HER FEAR AND DESPAIR INTO HER POLITICAL DRAWINGS...

(*Garm* magazine, 1938)

...AND IMAGINES A FAMILY OF PEACEFUL CREATURES FORCED TO LEAVE THEIR HOME WHEN A COMET THREATENS TO ANNIHILATE THEIR BEAUTIFUL VALLEY.

THE YEAR IS 1945; THESE ARE THE MOOMINS, AND THEY WILL GO ON TO CHANGE TOVE'S LIFE.

INITIALLY INTENDED AS A SIDE HOBBY, THESE ILLUSTRATED BOOKS ARE INSPIRED BY HER HAPPY CHILDHOOD.

The Moomins explore enchanting islands.

Moominmamma is free and encourages her kids to live life the same way (and to smoke).

Their friend, crazy Little My, represents Tove as a child.

THOUGH THESE STORIES ARE INTENDED FOR CHILDREN, THE MOOMIN ADVENTURES ARE ALSO ABOUT HER LIFE.

Any still life, any landscape— it is all just a self-portrait.

FOR EXAMPLE, THESE ARE HER CHARACTERS THINGUMY AND BOB.

THEY ALWAYS WALK AROUND HOLDING HANDS AND CARRY WITH THEM A SUITCASE: A SECRET THEY CAN'T TELL ANYONE.

HOMOSEXUALITY IS ILLEGAL IN FINLAND AT THIS TIME, AND TOVE IS IN A SECRET RELATIONSHIP WITH A MARRIED WOMAN.

(THE SUITCASE IN QUESTION CONTAINS A MAGNIFICENT RUBY, WHICH PEOPLE ARE CONSTANTLY TRYING TO STEAL FROM THINGUMY AND BOB.)

TOVE'S BOOKS ARE A HIT, AND SHE SETS UP HER ART STUDIO IN A SMALL TOWER.

A dream come true!

TOVE'S PAINTINGS AND DRAWINGS ARE WIDELY EXHIBITED AND READERS DISCOVER HER ELEGANT AND INCREDIBLY EXPRESSIVE LINE.

Cheers!

(first solo show, 1950)

A NEWSPAPER IN ENGLAND ASKS HER TO CREATE A MOOMINS COMIC STRIP.

WITHOUT REALLY KNOWING WHAT SHE'S GETTING HERSELF INTO, TOVE SAYS YES.

Tove.

SHE IS MET WITH INSTANT (AND, SHORTLY AFTER, INTERNATIONAL) SUCCESS. ALL THE PAPERS FIGHT FOR THE CHANCE TO SYNDICATE THE MOOMINS, WHOSE ADVENTURES ARE READ BY TWELVE MILLION PEOPLE AROUND THE WORLD.

Six comic strips a week....

...for *seven years.*

TOVE STOPS DOING ANYTHING ELSE. SHE DOESN'T PAINT ANYMORE, DOESN'T WRITE... SHE IS CALLED "MOMMY MOOMINS."

BETWEEN DREAMING UP IDEAS EVERY DAY AND READING HER FAN MAIL (WHICH SHE ANSWERS PERSONALLY)...

Dear Moomin,

...TOVE IS NOW WORKING EXCLUSIVELY FOR NEWSPAPERS. SHE IS MISERABLE AND COMES TO HATE THE MOOMINS.

WALT DISNEY OFFERS TO BUY THE MOOMIN FAMILY FROM HER.

(SHE SENDS HIM PACKING.)

TOVE IS IN FULL DEPRESSION MODE WHEN, AT A PARTY ONE NIGHT, SHE MEETS FELLOW FINNISH ARTIST TUULIKKI PIETILÄ.

SHE INVITES HER TO DANCE. (SCANDALOUS!)

IT'S LOVE AT FIRST SIGHT, AND THEY BECOME LIFE PARTNERS.

Too-Ticky, a new character in Moomin's adventures (who guides him through the winter)

TOVE AND TUULIKKI DREAM OF ISOLATION AND LIFE IN THE WILD.

THEY BUILD A HOUSE (WITH NO ELECTRICITY) ON AN ISLAND, AND MAKE THEIR RETREAT AS FAST AS THEY CAN.

USING DRIFTWOOD, THEY BUILD TEMPORARY CONSTRUCTIONS THAT ARE SWEPT AWAY BY THE STORMS.

EVEN THEIR SECLUDED ISLAND IS BESIEGED BY FANS.

Look!!! It's Mommy Moomins!

IN 1970, TOVE LOSES HER MOTHER.

DEVASTATED, SHE DECIDES TO PEN THE LAST MOOMINS BOOK.

After that, let's go away. Far away. For a long time.

ON THEIR TRIP AROUND THE WORLD, TOVE FINALLY RELAXES.

SHE STARTS WRITING FOR HER OWN PLEASURE, WITH NO ENDGAME IN MIND.

THE MOOMINS BRAND IS THRIVING: FIFTEEN MILLION BOOKS SOLD, MOVIES, TOYS...

SO TOVE DECIDES TO DELEGATE AS MUCH RESPONSIBILITY AS POSSIBLE TO HER BROTHER LARS (WHO WRITES THE STORIES FROM THERE ON OUT)...

...AND SHE SPENDS THE REST OF HER DAYS WRITING, PAINTING, SMOKING, TRAVELING, AND ENJOYING TUULIKKI.

JUST LIKE THE MOOMINS, THEY MAKE CREPES, GO ON PICNICS, TELL STORIES, AND TAKE CARE OF EACH OTHER...

...AS IF NOTHING ELSE REALLY MATTERS THAT MUCH.

THEIR LAST TRIP TAKES THEM TO PARIS.

TOVE AND TUULIKKI PASS AWAY, RESPECTIVELY, AT THE AGES OF EIGHTY-SIX AND NINETY-TWO. (TOVE DIES OF LUNG CANCER.)

THOUGH SHE CREATED AN EMPIRE AND TO DATE REMAINS FINLAND'S MOST POPULAR ARTIST...

FINNAIR

...TOVE JANSSON NEVER LOST SIGHT OF HER PRIORITIES.

"Only passion— hope and joy—can be honest. Nothing I've been forced to do has ever brought joy to me or those around me."

Pénélope

AGNODICE

GYNECOLOGIST

~350 AV.J.-C.

AGNODICE IS BORN IN ATHENS, IN THE FOURTH CENTURY BC.

AS A CHILD, SHE WITNESSES WOMEN IN HER FAMILY SUFFER (AND DIE) IN CHILDBIRTH...

...USUALLY BECAUSE THEY TRY TO MANAGE THINGS THEMSELVES...

...RATHER THAN CALL ON A (MALE) PHYSICIAN FOR HELP.

YOU SEE, THE ATHENIANS HAD RECENTLY BARRED WOMEN FROM PRACTICING MEDICINE, AS THEY SUSPECTED THEY WERE PROVIDING ABORTIONS.

I mean really!

Those witches!

We'd just as soon watch them die!

(THUS DESTROYING THE BOND THAT ONCE EXISTED BETWEEN WOMEN DOCTORS AND THEIR PATIENTS.)

Now, now, no fidgeting! Open wide!

YOUNG AGNODICE IS OUTRAGED BY THE ABSURD SITUATION.

"Not allowed"??

We'll see about that!

UNIVERSITY OF ATH

SNACK BAR

UNDER THE GUISE OF VISITING A SICK FRIEND, SHE TAKES OFF ON A LONG VOYAGE.

Don't go talking to strangers!

BUT IN REALITY, SHE GOES TO EGYPT...

...WHERE WOMEN ARE ALLOWED TO STUDY MEDICINE.

What'd you put down for number eight?

"Liver ablation." You?

WITH SOLID (AND SECRETIVE) TRAINING UNDER HER BELT, SHE RETURNS TO GREECE, FULLY DETERMINED TO HELP THE WOMEN OF ATHENS.

Right... that's all well and good, but I still can't legally work.

SHE MUST RESORT TO DRESSING UP AS A MAN.

AT FIRST, SHE ENCOUNTERS THE SAME RETICENCE AS HER MALE COLLEAGUES.

Just trust me, okay?

BUT ONE DAY, SHE SAVES THE LIFE OF A PATIENT...

And voila!

...WHO TELLS ALL HER GIRLFRIENDS ABOUT HER ONE-OF-A-KIND DOC.

WORD GETS AROUND AND AGNODICE QUICKLY BECOMES *THE* GO-TO OB-GYN IN ATHENS.

THE OTHER PHYSICIANS ARE A LITTLE IRKED BY THE UNUSUAL MONOPOLY...

...AND EVENTUALLY ACCUSE AGNODICE OF SEDUCING HER MARRIED PATIENTS.

Of *what?!!*

SHE IS TRIED BY A TRIBUNAL OF HUSBANDS AND DOCTORS.

Very well.

You asked for it.

AGNODICE HAS NO CHOICE BUT TO PROVIDE IRREFUTABLE EVIDENCE OF HER INNOCENCE.

NOW EVEN MORE OUTRAGED (AND HUMILIATED, MOSTLY, FOR HAVING BEEN DUPED), THEY SENTENCE HER TO DEATH FOR PRACTICING MEDICINE ILLEGALLY.

JUST THEN, A LARGE GROUP OF ANGRY PATIENTS SHOWS UP. THEY CHASTISE THEIR HUSBANDS AND TELL THE DOCTORS IT WAS THEIR OWN FAULT FOR BEING SO LAME.

ASHAMED OF THEMSELVES, THE MEN EVENTUALLY ACQUIT THE ACCUSED...

...AND LEGALIZE WOMEN DOCTORS AGAIN IN ATHENS.

LEYMAH GBOWEE

SOCIAL WORKER

1972-

IN THE GBOWEE FAMILY, BABY NUMBER FOUR IS BORN ON FEBRUARY 1, 1972.

Another girl.

HER MOTHER NAMES HER LEYMAH (WHICH MEANS "WHAT IS WRONG WITH ME?").

BUT EARLY ON, PEOPLE START CALLING HER "RED" ON ACCOUNT OF HER LIGHT SKIN.

AT HOME, THE FAMILY LIVES WITH HER GRANDMOTHER. SHE'S A BIT OF A WITCH AND DELIVERS THE BABIES OF THE WOMEN WHO ARE TOO POOR TO GO TO THE HOSPITAL. (RUMOR HAS IT THAT SHE CAN HYPNOTIZE SNAKES.)

LEYMAH'S PARENTS FIGHT CONSTANTLY, ESPECIALLY OVER HER FATHER'S INCESSANT INDISCRETIONS, BUT LEYMAH IS SPOILED BY HER SISTERS.

LIBERIA WAS FOUNDED BY FREED AMERICAN SLAVES, AND LEYMAH THEREFORE GROWS UP WITH A MIXED CULTURAL HERITAGE.

SHE IS FIRST IN HER CLASS AND PLANS ON GOING TO MED SCHOOL TO BECOME A DOCTOR. HER GOOD GRADES MEAN SHE CAN DO NO WRONG: HER PARENTS LET HER GO OUT, HIT THE DANCE CLUBS, DATE.

HER FIRST BOYFRIEND SLAPS HER IN PUBLIC.
(UPON WHICH SHE PROMPTLY DUMPS HIM.)

103

IN HER NEIGHBORHOOD LEYMAH HAS FRIENDS OF MANY DIFFERENT FAITHS. BUT THE COUNTRY IS IN THE THROES OF UNREST AND DRASTIC SOCIAL INEQUALITY.

① Between Liberians of American origins and the "natives"...

② ...and between the various tribes.

← The Krahn land all the good jobs.

← The Gio and the Mano have it rough.

IN 1989, A GROUP OF REBELS CALLED THE NPFL, LED BY CHARLES TAYLOR, ANNOUNCES THEY ARE SEIZING POWER AND KICKING OUT THE KRAHN. CIVIL WAR BREAKS OUT, WITH PEOPLE SHOOTING ONE ANOTHER IN THE STREETS.

TERRIFIED, LEYMAH AND HER MOTHER AND SISTERS RUN FOR SHELTER IN A CHURCH, LEAVING EVERYTHING BEHIND.

THE CITY IS GOING UP IN FLAMES. LEYMAH IS ONLY SEVENTEEN, BUT SHE KNOWS HER LITTLE TEENAGE PROBLEMS ARE OVER; SHE BECOMES AN ADULT OVERNIGHT.

THEY END UP IN A TEMPORARY REFUGEE CAMP IN GHANA, WHICH TURNS OUT TO BE NOT SO TEMPORARY.

Her mother refuses to give up, and sets up a makeshift home for them.

Leymah starts selling fritters.

MEN ARE CONSTANTLY CHECKING LEYMAH OUT.

ONE IN PARTICULAR HITS ON HER WITH NOTED PERSISTENCE. HE IS OLDER AND HIS NAME IS DANIEL. SHE FINDS HIM A LITTLE ODD (AND INTENSE), BUT HE BRINGS HER AND HER FAMILY A LOT OF GIFTS.

I'll walk you home.

HIS ATTENTION IS A RAY OF LIGHT TO HER WRETCHED EXISTENCE AND, WHAT'S MORE, IT MAKES HER FEEL A BIT LIKE A NORMAL YOUNG WOMAN.

Good night, Leymah.

SHE FALLS FOR HIM.

BUT DANIEL TURNS OUT TO BE THE JEALOUS TYPE...

...AND THEN THE VIOLENT TYPE.

WHAT DO YOU MEAN,"AT A FRIEND'S PLACE"?!!

HUH?!!

ONE DAY, HE STARTS HITTING HER.

LEYMAH DECIDES TO LEAVE HIM. BUT LIFE CHOOSES THAT VERY MOMENT TO THROW HER A LITTLE CURVEBALL.

BLEHHHHHHHHH

THE CIVIL WAR INTENSIFIES. JOSHUA IS BORN IN 1993.

THE BABY DOES LITTLE TO BRING OUT DANIEL'S SOFTER SIDE. HE BEATS LEYMAH EVEN HARDER AND RAPES HER ON A REGULAR BASIS.

BOOM! BOOM! BOOM!

Open up!!

LEYMAH FEELS TRAPPED. BUT MOSTLY, SHE FEELS PATHETIC. A TOTAL LOSER. AND TO THINK SHE WAS DESTINED FOR GREATNESS...

AS HER DESPAIR REACHES NEW DEPTHS, AND THE WAR RAGES ON, SHE BECOMES PREGNANT AGAIN.

105

SHE LEARNS THAT UNICEF IS OFFERING SOCIAL WORK TRAINING FOR WAR VICTIMS.

Sure, whatever.

Anything. to get me out of the house.

SHE BORROWS THE NECESSARY MONEY AND, DESPITE HER HUSBAND'S RESISTANCE (HE HAS JUST BEEN FIRED AND IS NURSING A BRUISED EGO), SHE BEGINS HER TRAINING.

AS FATE WOULD HAVE IT, SHE'S TRAINED TO HELP WOMEN WHO ARE VICTIMS OF VIOLENCE AND DOMESTIC ABUSE.

Break the circle of violence

SHE'S SENT INTO THE FIELD TO CARE FOR REFUGEES FROM SIERRA LEONE.

MOST OF THEM HAVE BEEN RAPED OR MUTILATED.

AND YET THEY ARE FEISTY. STRONG. THEY JOKE AROUND. THEY HAVE *HOPE*.

TEN TIMES MORE THAN LEYMAH HAS.

THE WOMEN THANK HER WHEN SHE LEAVES.

You did what no one wants to do: you *listened* to us.

LEYMAH REALIZES SHE'S ACTUALLY *GOOD AT SOMETHING*.

SHE STARTS WORKING IN THE FIELD MORE AND MORE, SOMETIMES LEAVING HER KIDS WITH HER SISTER. THE BEATINGS AT HOME GROW EVEN WORSE, BUT SHE DOESN'T CARE. NOW

SHE HAS
A
GOAL.

The girl I was at seventeen would *never* have accepted this life. It's *not* because of the war, it's *not* because of the kids. I am *not* worthless. I'm twenty-six, and I deserve better.

I am *strong*.

SHE GRABS HER KIDS AND LEAVES WITHOUT LOOKING BACK. JUST LIKE THAT.

(LITTLE DOES SHE KNOW, SHE'S PREGNANT AGAIN.)

SHE THROWS HERSELF INTO HER PEACEKEEPING MISSIONS, WHICH ENTAIL EMPOWERING VICTIMS AND, MOSTLY, GETTING THEM TO *TALK*.

Hi, my name is Leymah.

SHE REALIZES THAT WOMEN WERE THE FIRST VICTIMS OF THE CIVIL WAR: ONE OUT OF TWO HAD BEEN RAPED, THEIR SONS WERE RECRUITED AS CHILD SOLDIERS, THEY WALKED LONG MILES TO FEED THEIR FAMILIES...

...YET NOBODY LISTENS TO THEM OR INVOLVES THEM. EVER.

THEY SIT IN A CIRCLE AND TALK ABOUT THEIR ORDEAL BY THE LIGHT OF A CANDLE. (LEYMAH SHARES FIRST.)

We women must always put on a brave face.

Not here.

ON HER LONG MISSIONS, HER KIDS LIVE WITH HER SISTER. THEY TREAT HER LIKE A STRANGER WHENEVER SHE COMES HOME.

She brings along their sheets to keep their scent

IT'S HARD, BUT SHE KEEPS AT IT AND STUDIES FOR A DEGREE THAT WILL MEAN MORE RESPONSIBILITIES.

PLUS, SHE JUST LOVES TO LEARN.

AS PART OF HER TRAINING, SHE HELPS REHABILITATE CHILD SOLDIERS.

They are lost, violent drug addicts who are treated like pariahs (and whom everybody fears).

BUT LEYMAH HAS JUST WHAT IT TAKES.

I've got *four* bums like you at home, so *don't even think about it.*

AT A CONFERENCE IN GHANA, SHE MEETS HER ALTER EGO, THE HIGHLY EDUCATED THELMA EKIYOR. THOUGH WORLDS APART, THEY CLICK IMMEDIATELY.

TOGETHER, THEY COME UP WITH A PLAN TO INCLUDE WOMEN IN THE PEACE NEGOTIATIONS (WHICH HAS NEVER HAPPENED BEFORE).

THEY CALL IT

(The Women in Peacebuilding Network)

LEYMAH CUSTOM DESIGNS IT, MIXING WHAT SHE LEARNED IN BOOKS AND IN THE FIELD WITH A DASH OF MEDIATION, CONFIDENCE-BUILDING, AND EMPOWERING EXERCISES.

The UN gives us water and shelter, but you, Leymah, you do *so much more*.

IN THE STREETS, PEOPLE ARE SHOOTING CIVILIANS ON SIGHT. THERE'S A CURFEW IN EFFECT, AND A MASSACRE ON EVERY CORNER.

BUT LEYMAH GOES EVERYWHERE FEARLESSLY AND UNDETERRED.

SHE BELIEVES IN WOMEN'S POTENTIAL IF UNITED, AND SHE WORKS TO ORGANIZE THEM THROUGHOUT THE COUNTRY.

WOMEN OF LIBERIA: WAKE UP! —WIPNET—

SHE SCORES A BIG COUP WHEN SHE MANAGES TO BRING CHRISTIAN AND MUSLIM WOMEN TOGETHER TO DISCUSS PEACE.

We're *sisters*! And we're *sick* of this war!

ONLY MEN HAVE THE POWER TO STOP THE WAR. LEYMAH INCITES THE WOMEN OF LIBERIA TO GO ON A SEXUAL HUNGER STRIKE TO PUT PRESSURE ON THEIR HUSBANDS.

'Night!

FINALLY, THE PEACE TALKS BEGIN. LEYMAH STAGES A SIT-IN THAT BLOCKS EVERY EXIT. THE DELEGATES CAN'T LEAVE UNTIL THEY REACH AN AGREEMENT.

We're thirsty!

TOUGH LUCK!!

WOMEN BY THE THOUSANDS JOIN HER AND SIT OUTSIDE THE PRESIDENTIAL PALACE DRESSED IN WHITE. FROM ALL AGES, ALL FAITHS, AND ALL SOCIAL CLASSES. SOME WALK FOR DAYS TO BE THERE. OTHERS WEAR WHITE CURTAINS FOR LACK OF OPTIONS. BUT THEY ARE ALL THERE. AND THEY AREN'T LEAVING.

PEACE

WE ARE TIRED

WE WANT PEACE

LEYMAH IS EVENTUALLY INVITED TO THE NEGOTIATION TABLE (NEXT TO THE COUNTRY'S BIGGEST SCUMBAGS).

How about a drink?

I don't drink with murderers.

SHE FEELS HELPLESS AS SHE WITNESSES THE VICIOUS WARLORDS PROFIT FROM THEIR MAYHEM.

ENOUGH IS **ENOUGH.**

AFTER FOURTEEN YEARS OF WAR, LEYMAH'S PATIENCE IS WEARING THIN.

It's time for women to stop being *politely angry!!!*

EXHAUSTED AND DESPERATE, SHE THREATENS TO RIP OFF HER CLOTHES AND STAND THERE BUCK NAKED IN PROTEST (A VERY SERIOUS OFFENSE IN HER CULTURE).

THE EYES OF THE WORLD ARE NOW ON LIBERIA. INTERNATIONAL PRESSURE GROWS SO STRONG THAT LIBERIAN PRESIDENT CHARLES TAYLOR AGREES TO STEP DOWN ON AUGUST 11, 2003. (THEN HE EXILES HIMSELF IN NIGERIA—A BOLD MOVE.)

ELECTIONS ARE HELD TWO YEARS LATER. LEYMAH CAMPAIGNS HARD TO GET WOMEN, AS WELL AS THE POOR AND THE UNEDUCATED, TO VOTE.

ELLEN JOHNSON SIRLEAF IS ELECTED PRESIDENT OF LIBERIA—SHE IS THE FIRST FEMALE HEAD OF STATE IN AFRICA. SHE ASKS FOR TAYLOR TO BE EXTRADITED; HE'S LATER CONVICTED OF CRIMES AGAINST HUMANITY.

Whiny bitches.

LEYMAH FINISHES HER STUDIES IN AMERICA, BUT SHE REFUSES TO JOIN THE LIBERIAN GOVERNMENT.

I'm *much better* at teaching women how to come together to solve the problems of the world.

TODAY, SHE'S THE MOTHER OF SIX CHILDREN—ALL SELF-DESCRIBED FEMINISTS.

LEYMAH IS AWARDED THE NOBEL PEACE PRIZE IN 2011.

Penelope *

GIORGINA REID

LIGHTHOUSE KEEPER

1908-2001

GIORGINA ANZULATA IS BORN ON NOVEMBER 3, 1908, IN TRIESTE, ITALY...

...AND SAILS ACROSS THE ATLANTIC WITH HER MOTHER TO SETTLE IN AMERICA.

SHE IS VERY *INQUISITIVE*. SHE NEEDS TO UNDERSTAND EVERYTHING: HOW THINGS ARE MADE, HOW THEY WORK.

Eat your chicken, Gina!

SHE SPENDS ALL HER FREE TIME READING, INVENTING THINGS, AND PAINTING.

THE LEONARDO DA VINCI ART SCHOOL IN NEW YORK MAKES AN EXCEPTION FOR GIORGINA AND ALLOWS HER TO ENROLL DESPITE BEING ONLY FIFTEEN.

SHE MAJORS IN TEXTILE DESIGN AND MEETS HER FUTURE HUSBAND, DONALD REID, IN THE PROGRAM.

THEY MOVE TO QUEENS BUT DREAM OF THE SEA.

THEY SAVE UP THEIR WHOLE LIVES TO BUY A LITTLE HOUSE WITH A VIEW OF THE OCEAN.

THEY FINALLY PULL IT OFF, SETTLING IN THE CLIFFS OF ROCKY POINT, LONG ISLAND, WHERE THEY WILL LIVE OUT THE REST OF THEIR LIVES. BUT THE NEIGHBORS WARN THEM:

Unfortunately, all our houses will be under-water within ten years!

It's erosion!

114

SURE ENOUGH, A MERE TWO YEARS LATER, A STORM BATTERS THE COAST AND THE REIDS LOSE A FOOT OF GARDEN.

DONALD WANTS TO SELL. BUT GIORGINA REFUSES TO GIVE UP THEIR HOME. THEN SHE REMEMBERS SOMETHING SHE READ ABOUT AGES AGO.

I think it was in this one...

SHE SKETCHES OUT A PLAN BASED ON A JAPANESE GARDENING TECHNIQUE, COLLECTS DRIFTWOOD AND REEDS FROM THE BEACH, AND GETS TO WORK.

THIS IS WHAT SHE BUILDS:

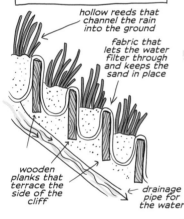

hollow reeds that channel the rain into the ground

fabric that lets the water filter through and keeps the sand in place

wooden planks that terrace the side of the cliff

drainage pipe for the water

THE FOLLOWING SUMMER, ROCKY POINT IS POUNDED BY MORE TORRENTIAL RAINS. THE REIDS' GARDEN IS THE ONLY ONE TO WITHSTAND THEM.

LONG ISLAND IS HOME TO ANOTHER VICTIM OF THE EROSION:

THE MONTAUK LIGHTHOUSE.

THE LIGHTHOUSE, LOCATED AT THE FAR TIP OF THE ISLAND, ON THE FRONT LINE OF THE OCEAN'S ATTACKS, HAS WITNESSED THE INEXORABLE SHRINKING OF THE COASTLINE SINCE THE TOWER WAS BUILT UNDER GEORGE WASHINGTON.

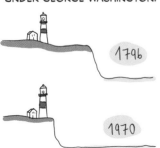

1796

1970

THE COAST GUARD TRIES TO STOP THE EROSION WITH ROCKS, BUT NOTHING DOING: THE COASTLINE KEEPS CRUMBLING. IN 1967, THEY SUFFER DRASTIC BUDGET CUTS. EXPENSIVE TO MAINTAIN AND OBSOLETE IN THE ERA OF AUTOMATED SIGNALS, THE MONTAUK LIGHTHOUSE IS DECOMMISSIONED. THE EASTERN DISTRICT GIVES UP AND ANNOUNCES IT WILL BE REPLACED BY A MODERN LIGHTHOUSE BUILT ON LAND SHELTERED FROM THE WAVES. THE OLD LIGHTHOUSE IS LEFT TO THE OCEAN'S FURY.

MONTAUK RESIDENTS ORGANIZE PROTESTS, "LIGHT-INS," IN FRONT OF THE LIGHTHOUSE TO CONVINCE THE AUTHORITIES TO TRY TO SAVE IT.

BUT THE DIE HAS BEEN CAST.

THE SITUATION SEEMS HOPELESS, UNTIL ONE DAY IN 1970, WHEN A FOUR-FOOT-ELEVEN LADY SHOWS UP IN THE COAST GUARD'S OFFICE LOOKING VERY DETERMINED.

I have a plan.

ALTHOUGH SKEPTICAL AT FIRST, THEY FIGURE THIS LITTLE OLD LADY IS FAIRLY HARMLESS.

And how much is this little plan of yours going to cost?

Nothing at all.

THE COAST GUARD APPROVES THE BUDGET AND GREENLIGHTS THE PROJECT.

ON APRIL 22, 1970, WITH THE HELP OF HER HUSBAND, A FEW ROCKY POINT RETIREES, AND SOME LOCAL YOUNGSTERS, GIORGINA SETS OUT FOR TURTLE HILL ARMED WITH REEDS AND SANDBAGS.

SHE'S NO ENGINEER, BUT SHE HAS BEEN GIFTED WITH IMPRESSIVE PRACTICAL KNOW-HOW. SHE *JUST KNOWS*.

Further down, young man!

PATIENTLY, FOR HOURS, DAYS, WEEKS...

...THEY PLANT.

AFTER SPENDING A YEAR WATCHING THEM AND SCRATCHING THEIR HEADS, THE COAST GUARD DECIDES TO LEND A HAND.

It's okay, we can manage.

But providing the materials would be a huge help.

RELENTLESSLY, TERRACE AFTER TERRACE, GIORGINA TRANSFORMS THE CLIFF (EVEN WHEN SHE BREAKS HER LEG). SURROUNDED BY DOZENS OF VOLUNTEERS ON SUNNY DAYS...

...OR ALL BY HERSELF ON RAINY ONES.

EVERY SUNDAY.

FOR FIFTEEN YEARS.

IN 1985, GIORGINA'S WORK IS DONE.

THE LIGHTHOUSE IS FINALLY SAFE, AND THE COAST GUARD ORGANIZES A CEREMONY HONORING ITS PROTECTOR.

ON THAT OCCASION, THEY READ HER A LETTER OF CONGRATULATIONS AND THANKS WRITTEN BY PRESIDENT RONALD REAGAN. GIORGINA WEEPS WITH JOY.

The historical society also awards her a badge of honor.

TODAY, THE MONTAUK POINT LIGHTHOUSE IS THE FOURTH OLDEST ACTIVE LIGHTHOUSE IN THE U.S. IT'S ALSO A HISTORIC MONUMENT OPEN TO TOURISTS.

$40

KEEP CALM AND VISIT MONTAUK

TOWARD THE END OF HER LIFE, GIORGINA SUFFERS FROM ALZHEIMER'S.

SHE CAN BARELY REMEMBER WHO THE U.S. PRESIDENT IS, BUT SHE CAN STILL EXPLAIN THE TERRACING IN THE TINIEST TECHNICAL DETAILS.

The drainage system is very important!

GIORGINA NEVER HAD CHILDREN.
("I did have one! The lighthouse!")

THE NURSE CARING FOR HER WAS ONE OF THE YOUNG VOLUNTEERS ON THE REID TEAM YEARS EARLIER.

SHE TAKES HER TO THE LIGHTHOUSE (NOW ALSO A MUSEUM) ONE LAST TIME, FOR THE INAUGURATION OF THE GIORGINA REID ROOM.

GIORGINA REID PASSES AWAY AT THE AGE OF NINETY-TWO. SHE IS BURIED NEXT TO HER HUSBAND, WITH HER BADGE FROM THE HISTORICAL SOCIETY.

GIORGINA REID
1908 - 2001
KEEPER OF THE LIGHT

Pénélope

CHRISTINE JORGENSEN
RELUCTANT CELEBRITY

1926-1989

THE JORGENSENS LIVE IN THE BRONX, IN NEW YORK CITY. ON MAY 30, 1926, THEY WELCOME THEIR SECOND CHILD...

...WHO, BY ALL APPEARANCES, IS A BOY. BUT AS IT TURNS OUT, THIS ISN'T THE CASE.

THEY NAME THEIR BABY GEORGE, JR.— BUT DEEP DOWN, GEORGE IS A GIRL.

GEORGE IS A VERY SLENDER CHILD WHO IS ALWAYS BEING PICKED ON.

HAVING TO WEAR BOYS' CLOTHES IS TORTURE FOR HER, AND SHE SECRETLY PUTS ON HER SISTER'S PRETTY DRESSES. SHE LONGS FOR A DOLL FOR CHRISTMAS ABOVE ALL ELSE.

Please, Baby Jesus.

I *hate* trains.

AS A TEEN, SHE QUICKLY BECOMES VERY JEALOUS OF HER BEST FRIEND.

OR RATHER, JEALOUS OF HIS GIRLFRIENDS.

GEORGE KEEPS TO HERSELF. SHE AVOIDS PARTIES, BECOMES AN INTROVERT, AND ENTERTAINS SERIOUSLY DARK THOUGHTS AT TIMES.

TO TAKE HER MIND OFF THINGS, HER FATHER TEACHES HER HOW TO DEVELOP FILM IN THEIR KITCHEN.

HER BEST FRIEND IS DRAFTED.

All right, man, see ya!

GEORGE ALMOST WISHES HE WON'T COME BACK, SO SHE CAN BE FREED FROM THE WEIGHT OF HER FEELINGS.

123

GEORGE IS DEEMED UNFIT FOR DUTY TWICE, BECAUSE OF HER BODY WEIGHT...

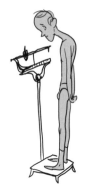

...BUT SHE'S EVENTUALLY DRAFTED IN THE ARMY, WHERE SHE SERVES ONE YEAR. LOST IN A SEA OF ANONYMITY, GEORGE GETS BY ALL RIGHT, AND ARMY LIFE ISN'T ALTOGETHER UNPLEASANT.

AFTER THE WAR, GEORGE TRIES HER HAND AT PHOTOGRAPHY BUT LACKS THE SELF-CONFIDENCE (SHE LITERALLY HATES HERSELF) TO ACTIVELY SOLICIT CLIENTS.

ONE MORNING, FEELING UTTERLY LOST, SHE GOES TO THE NEW YORK PUBLIC LIBRARY IN SEARCH OF ANY POSSIBLE ANSWER.

And also everything you have on glands and on hormones.

SHE READS EVERYTHING SHE CAN FIND, BUT LACKS MEDICAL KNOWLEDGE.

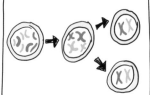

SHE DECIDES TO TAKE ADVANTAGE OF THE G.I. BILL (WHICH PROVIDES COLLEGE TUITION ASSISTANCE FOR DISCHARGED SOLDIERS) AND TO TRAIN IN BIOLOGY.

AFTER A FEW MONTHS OF CLASSES, SHE BEGINS TO FORMULATE A THEORY.

Professor! Let's imagine... Er... So for example, um... If a man were to receive female hormo

Impossible.

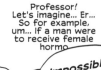

BUT GEORGE HAS NOTHING TO LOSE, SO SHE BEGINS MIXING UP A HOMEMADE HORMONE THERAPY, ALL ALONE IN HER ROOM.

Okay. Let's give it a shot.

(SHE MAKES HERSELF VERY SICK IN THE PROCESS.)

A DOCTOR FRIEND OF HERS GROWS CONCERNED ABOUT HER HEALTH.

First: stop that nonsense. Second: go to where people care about this stuff...

...Denmark.

SHE MAKES UP HER MIND. SHE THROWS A LITTLE FAREWELL PARTY FOR FAMILY AND FRIENDS BUT REMAINS EVASIVE ABOUT THE DETAILS OF HER TRIP.

To the George you know! Say good-bye to him, sis!

SHE ARRIVES IN COPENHAGEN AT THE AGE OF TWENTY-THREE.

THE MAN WHO CAN SUPPOSEDLY HELP HER IS DR. CHRISTIAN HAMBURGER, THE HEAD OF ENDOCRINOLOGY AT THE STATENS SERUM INSTITUT.

Hello, my name is George and I would like to know what is wrong with me.

SHE TELLS HIM EVERYTHING: HER DESPAIR, THE SEXUAL "NO MAN'S LAND" BETWEEN GENDERS IN WHICH SHE FEELS LIKE SHE IS DYING, AND HER CONVICTION THAT WHAT OTHERS SEE ISN'T HER TRUE SELF.

AND THE DOC *LISTENS*.

HE DOESN'T JUDGE HER. HE BARELY LOOKS SURPRISED.

You have the *sexual features* of a boy.

You were *registered* as a boy.

But it does look like somewhere in there, you're a woman, that's all.

GEORGE THEN AGREES TO BECOME DR. HAMBURGER'S GUINEA PIG AND EMBARKS ON AN INTENSE THREE-YEAR HORMONE THERAPY.

You realize, George, it could be dangerous, right?

Yes, but either way, I can't go on living like this.

UNDER CLOSE MONITORING FROM THE DOC AND A SHRINK, GEORGE WATCHES HER BODY AND FACE TRANSFORM. SHE LEARNS TO MODIFY HER VOICE.

Hello?

Yes, it's me, I swear.

THE DOC THEN SUGGESTS A SURGERY. THE RESULT: HER BODY WILL STOP PRODUCING MALE HORMONES. THIS REQUIRES THE AUTHORIZATION OF THE DANISH MINISTER OF JUSTICE.

Let's do this!

THE OPERATION IS PERFORMED, BUT GEORGE WANTS OFFICIAL RECOGNITION. SO SHE MEETS WITH THE U.S. AMBASSADOR AND ASKS HIM TO CHANGE HER PASSPORT AND HER FIRST NAME.

Christine.

As a tribute to the best doctor in the world, Dr. Christian.

GEORGE HAS ALWAYS BEEN A WOMAN, BUT NOW CHRISTINE IS A WOMAN IN THE EYES OF EVERYBODY ELSE. HER NEW NAME CHANGES HER LIFE.

She finally dares to dress as she pleases

(using a DIY approach, as she is flat broke).

HER FIRST PUBLIC OUTING IS A TRIP TO THE BEAUTY SALON WITH HER GIRLFRIENDS.

I... I've never been happier in my life.

CHRISTINE FEELS BEAUTIFUL. STRONG. SURE OF HERSELF. SHE FINDS WORK AS A PHOTOGRAPHER AND EVEN MAKES A FILM.

SHE TELLS DR. HAMBURGER SHE'S READY FOR ANOTHER OPERATION. BUT FIRST, IT'S TIME TO WRITE HER FAMILY A LONG LETTER.

Remember the shy, miserable person who left America? Well, that person is no more. Nature made a mistake, and I corrected it. I am your daughter.

C.

BUT A REPORTER WITH THE *NEW YORK DAILY NEWS*, HUNGRY FOR A JUICY SCANDAL, TRICKS THE JORGENSENS TO GET HIS HANDS ON THAT LETTER AND USES IT TO PEN A SENSATIONAL, REDUCTIVE, AND PARTIALLY UNTRUE ARTICLE.

EX G.I. BECOMES BLONDE BEAUTY

George Jr. before incredible operation transformed ...in Denmark

WHEN SHE AWAKES FROM ANOTHER SURGERY, A STUNNED CHRISTINE FINDS PILES OF TELEGRAMS AND REQUESTS FOR INTERVIEWS.

For you again. What do I tell them?

HER PARENTS, CLEVERLY AVOIDING THE PAPARAZZI, COME TO VISIT HER IN COPENHAGEN, FINALLY SEEING THEIR DAUGHTER AGAIN AFTER YEARS APART.

You're so pretty.

THE REUNION GIVES CHRISTINE THE COURAGE TO RETURN TO THE U.S. WITH HER HEAD HELD HIGH.

HUNDREDS OF REPORTERS ARE WAITING FOR HER ON THE TARMAC IN NEW YORK.

Christine! Christine! Christine! Christine! Christine!

CHRISTINE WOULD HAVE PREFERRED A LOW PROFILE, BUT SINCE THE WORLD WANTS TO SEE HER AND HEAR HER, SHE USES HER NEW PLATFORM TO HELP ALL THOSE SUFFERING AS SHE DID.

The ridicule and the emotional torture must stop now.

AT THE HEIGHT OF THE COLD WAR, AMERICANS WERE FASCINATED BY SCIENCE'S VICTORY OVER NATURE.

CHRISTINE IS A SYMBOL OF THE FUTURE.

MEDIA OUTLETS FIGHT OVER HER; SHE PATIENTLY AGREES TO ALL INTERVIEWS. NEWSPAPERS ARE FLOODED BY FAN MAIL FROM ANONYMOUS PEN PALS RELIEVED TO LEARN THEY AREN'T ALONE. CHRISTINE ANSWERS AND COUNSELS THEM.

Nobody is 100% "man" or 100% "woman"...

SHE ISN'T THE FIRST TO DO WHAT SHE'S DONE, BUT NOBODY IN THE U.S. HAS EVER GONE PUBLIC WITH IT.

AMERICAN WEEKLY

WHO IS CHRISTINE JORGENSEN?

AND FOR THE PRESS, CHRISTINE IS THE PERFECT SUBJECT: HER BEAUTY AND COURAGE ARE PRAISED. SHE'S COMPLETELY *VALIDATED*.

ALL SHE WANTS IS A QUIET LIFE, BUT SHE FEELS IT IS HER DUTY TO USE HER POPULARITY FOR GOOD: SHE EDUCATES THE PRESS, GIVES SPEECHES AT UNIVERSITIES, AND EVEN WRITES A BOOK ABOUT HER STORY:

Christine

(IT SELLS 500,000 COPIES.)

THREE YEARS LATER, HER AUTOBIOGRAPHY COMES TO THE BIG SCREEN. DESPITE HER REQUESTS (SHE WAS A CONSULTANT ON THE FILM), THE STUDIO REFUSES TO CAST A WOMAN IN HER ROLE.

That's just *ridiculous!!*

IN 1959, HER LOVER PROPOSES TO HER, BUT THE NEW YORK CITY CLERK DENIES THEM A MARRIAGE LICENSE BECAUSE OF THE NAME "GEORGE JR." ON HER BIRTH CERTIFICATE.

I am so *humiliated*.

REPORTERS BECOME INCREASINGLY INVASIVE, ASKING CHRISTINE QUESTIONS THEY WOULD NEVER DARE ASK OTHER WOMEN.

Do you get periods?

Did you keep that little bit the surgeon chopped off as a memento?

THE FASCINATION WITH CHRISTINE DETERIORATES, AND SHE EVENTUALLY BECOMES A SIDESHOW ATTRACTION IN LAS VEGAS. BUT SHE ALWAYS KEEPS HER DIGNITY, LIKE THE TIME SHE'S ASKED ON LIVE TV ABOUT THE ROMANCE WITH HER "WIFE."

(SHE WALKS OFF THE SET, LEAVING THE SHOW'S HOST BUMBLING AND EMBARRASSED.)

STORIES ON THE BRAVE, GLAMOROUS WOMAN STOP SELLING, SO THE PRESS CHANGES ITS ANGLE, TURNING MEAN (AND DUMB): "TRANSVESTITE," "DEGENERATE," ETC. MAGAZINES START TO USE THE PRONOUN "HE" TO REFER TO CHRISTINE.

Wow.

I guess the enlightened tolerance phase is over.

AS IT TURNS OUT, SOCIETY HAS A HARD TIME ACCEPTING THE SPECTRUM OF IDENTITIES BETWEEN "MAN" AND "WOMAN."

So *what* is he, exactly?

It's unclear!

CHRISTINE MAKES PEOPLE UNCOMFORTABLE.

BUT THE PRESS STILL SPILLS A LOT OF INK OVER HER...

hush hush!

EXCLUSIVE!!

CHRISTINE: "I WANT TO BE A MAN AGAIN!!"

Shocking revelations from her inner circle (p. 3)

...AND SHE FIGURES THAT IF SHE HAS TO BE MOCKED TO BE HEARD, SO BE IT.

CHRISTINE FACES IT ALL WITH GREAT COURAGE. SHE RESPONDS WITH POISE AND PATIENCE. DESPITE THE FEAR AND HATRED SHE AROUSES, SHE GOES ON SERVING AS THE PUBLIC FACE OF ALL THOSE LIVING IN THE SHADOWS.

My body doesn't matter. I am a *woman* because I *want* to be.

SHE ATTENDS FANCY CHARITY EVENTS, IS ELECTED "WOMAN OF THE YEAR" BY A SCANDINAVIAN FOUNDATION...

...AND LIVES THE LIFE OF A SOCIALITE.

TO SUCH A POINT THAT ONE DAY AN AGENT SUGGESTS SHE TAKES TO THE STAGE.

Who

ME??

AND THIS IS HOW CHRISTINE ENDS UP AT FREDDY'S SUPPER CLUB IN MANHATTAN, BELTING OUT "I ENJOY BEING A GIRL" AT SOLD-OUT SHOWS.

IN LAS VEGAS, THE SAHARA HOTEL BOOKS HER FOR A SERIES OF CONCERTS, BUT LATER GETS COLD FEET. THEY ARGUE THAT HER CONTRACT IS VOID BECAUSE "SHE" IS REALLY A "HE."

THE GUILD OF VARIETY ARTISTS COMES TO HER RESCUE AND MAKES THE CASINO PAY CHRISTINE HER $12,000 WEEKLY FEE.

HER SINGING CAREER AFFORDS HER A COMFORTABLE LIFESTYLE IN CALIFORNIA, WHERE SHE WILL BE ABLE TO SPEND THE REST OF HER DAYS.

TOWARD THE END OF HER LIFE, SHE DEMANDS AN APOLOGY FROM VICE-PRESIDENT SPIRO AGNEW, WHO INSULTS A RIVAL POLITICIAN BY CALLING HIM THE

Christine Jorgensen of Republicans.

HA HA HA HA HA HA

MINDSETS ARE GRADUALLY EVOLVING, AND SHE'S THRILLED.

If I transitioned today, nobody would give a damn!

It's become banal!

AT THE AGE OF SIXTY-TWO, SHE LOSES HER BATTLE WITH CANCER OF THE BLADDER—PERHAPS A CONSEQUENCE OF THE HIGHLY EXPERIMENTAL THERAPY SHE TRIED FOR YEARS. HER ASHES ARE SCATTERED OVER THE OCEAN BY HER NIECE AND FRIENDS.

AT THE RISK OF BECOMING AN ODDITY, CHRISTINE CREATED A PUBLIC PERSONA THAT WAS AVAILABLE AND PLAYFUL, YET ALWAYS KNEW HOW TO ELICIT RESPECT AND CALMLY ASSERT HER RIGHT TO BE A WOMAN...

Kisses, haters!

...AND HER RIGHT TO LIVE WITH DIGNITY WHILE UNDER CONSTANT SCRUTINY.

SHE TOOK ON THE GREAT CHALLENGE OF BECOMING A PUBLIC FIGURE AND ENCOURAGED OTHERS TO DARE TO BE THEMSELVES.

I may not have initiated the sexual revolution, but I certainly gave it a good, swift kick in the pants.

WU ZETIAN

EMPRESS

624 - 705

LITTLE WU ZHAO IS BORN ON FEBRUARY 17, IN A YEAR MARKED BY A TOTAL ECLIPSE OF THE SUN.

HER FATHER IS A SICHUAN NOBLE WHO ENCOURAGES HER TO READ AS MUCH POSSIBLE.

CONFUCIUS

EARLY ON, WU DISPLAYS A RARE INTELLIGENCE AND LITERARY PALATE FOR SOMEONE SO YOUNG.

Hello-o!
I'm *Plato*...
Obviously!!

AND SINCE SHE'S EXCEPTIONALLY BEAUTIFUL TO BOOT, AT THE TENDER AGE OF TWELVE, WU FINDS HERSELF USHERED INTO THE MOST GLAMOROUS CAREER POSSIBLE FOR A WOMAN OF HER ERA...

...CONCUBINE TO THE EMPEROR.

Oh.

SHE BECOMES *CAIREN*, AKA A FIFTH-RANK CONSORT TO TAIZONG THE GREAT. BIG WHOOP.

ONE DAY, SHE MANAGES TO TAME A HORSE SAID TO BE UNTAMABLE, WHICH ATTRACTS THE ATTENTION OF THE EMPEROR, WHO HADN'T TAKEN MUCH NOTICE OF HER BEFORE.

I hear you can write, too?

In five languages.

Why?

HE UPGRADES HER TO *MEINIANG* ("CHARMING LADY"), WHICH BASICALLY MEANS SHE BECOMES HIS SECRETARY. HER NOSE IS BURIED IN OFFICIAL DOCUMENTS AND AFFAIRS OF STATE ALL DAY LONG.

THERE IS ONE WHO TAKES NOTICE OF HER FROM DAY ONE: THE EMPEROR'S SON GAOZONG.

THE EMPEROR DIES IN 649. TRADITION DEMANDS THAT IMPERIAL CONSORTS BE SHIPPED OFF TO A MONASTERY WHERE THEY WILL WHILE AWAY THE REST OF THEIR DAYS.

GAOZONG, WHO, IN THE MEANTIME, HAS BECOME THE (MARRIED) EMPEROR, KEEPS VISITING WU FOR THREE YEARS...

...UNTIL HE FINALLY MANAGES TO GET HER BACK INTO THE PALACE AS HIS CONCUBINE (AFTER BEING HIS FATHER'S CONCUBINE, WHICH CAUSES QUITE A SCANDAL...

...ESPECIALLY WITH EMPRESS WANG AND THE OFFICIAL CONCUBINE, XIAOSHU).

THINGS GROW EVEN TENSER FOR WU WHEN SHE GIVES BIRTH TO GAOZONG'S FIRST SON— IN OTHER WORDS, THE FUTURE EMPEROR.

(BUT SHE HASN'T COME THIS FAR JUST TO LET A BUNCH OF JEALOUS SHREWS STAB HER IN THE BACK.)

SOON THEREAFTER, WU ALSO GIVES BIRTH TO A DAUGHTER. TRAGICALLY, THE BABY SUFFOCATES TO DEATH, PERHAPS DUE TO A COMBINATION OF COAL FURNACES AND POOR VENTILATION IN THE PALACE.*

*Some historians have suggested that Wu strangled her own child, which is really pretty preposterous.

WU ACCUSES HER ENEMIES OF KILLING HER BABY, AKA THE BABY OF THE EMPEROR—WHO BELIEVES HER.

THEY ARE HUNTED DOWN AND EXECUTED.

WU AND GAOZONG ARE FINALLY MARRIED.

NOW CLOSE TO THE DECISION-MAKING CIRCLES, WU IS ALWAYS FULL OF IDEAS ON IMPORTANT MATTERS AND CAN'T HELP MEDDLING.

You're not seriously going to ratify *that?!!*

DAY AND NIGHT.

You know, I was thinking about that whole lowering the taxes thing and I

SHE AND THE EMPEROR GRADUALLY BECOME KNOWN AS THE "TWO SAGES," AND THEY RULE OVER CHINA TOGETHER. BUT IN 660, GAOZONG BEGINS TO HAVE FITS OF PARALYSIS, AND WU IS OFTEN CALLED ON TO GOVERN THE EMPIRE IN HIS STEAD.

HER POWER AND AUTHORITY ARE NOT LOOKED ON FONDLY BY MEMBERS OF THE IMPERIAL COURT, WHO ARE OUTRAGED TO HAVE TO OBEY A WOMAN (A "HEN WHO CROWS AT DAWN").

PEOPLE START TO SECRETLY CONSPIRE AGAINST THE EMPEROR'S TROUBLESOME WIFE.

A WORRIED WU CREATES A SORT OF SECRET POLICE FOR HERSELF TO TRACK DOWN HER ENEMIES, MANY OF WHOM END UP IN PRISON (OR WORSE).

WHEN GAOZONG DIES, THEIR OLDEST SON SUCCEEDS HIM.

BUT WU FINDS HIM PRETTY WORTHLESS...

...SO SHE MANAGES TO SIT HER YOUNGEST SON ON THE THRONE INSTEAD. THOUGH JUST AS WORTHLESS IN HER EYES, HE'S EASIER TO MANIPULATE.

CLAIMING THAT HE HAS A SPEECH IMPEDIMENT, WU SPEAKS FOR HIM (AND SAYS WHATEVER THE HECK SHE PLEASES).

IN 690, THEY DROP THE ACT: HE ABDICATES AND LEAVES MOMMY IN POWER.

WU ZETIAN ASCENDS THE THRONE OFFICIALLY. SHE BECOMES **SHENGSHEN**, THE FIRST (AND ONLY) WOMAN WITH THE TITLE OF EMPRESS REGNANT IN THE HISTORY OF CHINA.

AGAINST EVERYONE'S ADVICE, SHE FOUNDS HER OWN DYNASTY TO DISTINGUISH HERSELF FROM HER LATE HUSBAND'S: THE ZHOU DYNASTY, THE SHORTEST-LIVED ONE IN HISTORY (690-705).

RIGHT ABOUT THAT TIME, THE NOBLES, THE POLITICIANS, THE OLD BOYS' CLUB, AND PRETTY MUCH ALL THE OFFICIALS START TO HATE HER.

THEIR TROUBLES ARE JUST BEGINNING, SINCE FROM THEN ON, THE EMPRESS **ONLY** MAKES DECISIONS SURE TO IRRITATE THEM.

FIRST, SHE CLEANS HOUSE: SHE GETS RID OF THE MOST CORRUPT OFFICIALS AND MAKES THE PENCIL PUSHERS TAKE TESTS TO PROVE THEY KNOW WHAT THEY ARE DOING.

IN THE COUNTRYSIDE, FOR EXAMPLE, THEY ARE EVALUATED ON THEIR ABILITY TO FARM THE LAND.

CONVINCED THAT SUCH A MERITOCRACY WOULD BENEFIT FROM NEW BLOOD, WU ENCOURAGES ALL PEOPLE WHO FEEL DRIVEN TO DO SO TO ENGAGE IN POLITICAL LIFE, REGARDLESS OF THEIR SOCIAL STANDING.

What? Is this a *joke?!!*

TO PUT A STOP TO FAVORITISM, THE EMPRESS INTERVIEWS CANDIDATES FOR HER ADMINISTRATION HERSELF (WHICH IS UNHEARD OF).

My greatest flaw? I would say "perfectionism."

THAT'S HOW SHE DISCOVERS PROMISING NEW TALENT, SUCH AS HER PRIME MINISTER.

IN ORDER TO RESTORE WOMEN'S PLACE IN SOCIETY, WHICH CONFUCIANISM HAS DONE A SERIOUS NUMBER ON, SHE PAYS SCHOLARS TO WRITE BIOGRAPHIES OF GREAT WOMEN IN HISTORY.

SHE ALSO SIGNS TWELVE DECREES PROMOTING WOMEN'S SOCIAL POSITION, EDUCATION, RIGHTS, AND ACCESS TO GOVERNMENT OFFICES (KNOWING THAT SHE'S PRETTY MUCH STARTING FROM SCRATCH).

CONTEXT: IN THESE DAYS, EUROPEAN WOMEN ARE TREATED AS PERPETUAL CHILDREN. THEY DON'T ENJOY THE RIGHTS THAT ADULT MEN DO.

SHE INFLUENCES THE SPREAD OF BUDDHISM BY FUNDING HUGE SCULPTURE PROJECTS. THIS IS DONE AT THE EXPENSE OF HER WAR BUDGET, AS SHE HAS REDUCED THE MILITARY TO ITS BARE MINIMUM.

ABOVE ALL, HER EFFORTS ARE AIMED AT IMPROVING THE LIVING CONDITIONS OF FARMERS (AND LOWERING THE TAXES THEY ARE FORCED TO PAY). ESSENTIALLY, SHE DRAFTS SOME OF THE WORLD'S FIRST LABOR LAWS.

IN SHORT: SHE MAKES HER SHARE OF ENEMIES.

TOWARD THE END OF HER LIFE, SHE GROWS TIRED AND HUMBLY CEDES POWER TO HER SON, WHO PROMPTLY RESTORES HIS FATHER'S DYNASTY, AS IF HIS MOTHER'S LEGACY HAD NEVER HAPPENED.

← (Until the very end, she has lovers, namely two brothers fifty years her junior.)

WU PASSES AWAY AT EIGHTY-ONE. TRADITION HOLDS THAT ONE'S SUCCESSORS MUST SUM UP THE DECEASED'S LIFE ON HER TOMBSTONE.

TO THIS DAY, NO ONE HAS FIGURED OUT WHAT TO WRITE.

OFFICIAL HISTORIANS HAVE LONG DEPICTED WU ZETIAN AS A SORT OF CHINESE VERSION OF THE QUEEN OF HEARTS IN *ALICE IN WONDERLAND*, BY FOCUSING ON HER SECRET POLICE AND HER FONDNESS FOR BUMPING OFF ENEMIES.

Plus, she slept her way to the top!

AN INTERESTING ANGLE TO BE SURE, GIVEN THAT HER BRIEF DYNASTY WAS ONE OF CHINA'S MOST PROSPEROUS PERIODS IN MANY RESPECTS (IN TERMS OF PEACE, ARTS, AND SOCIAL PROGRESS).

ON THE OTHER HAND, WHAT'S ALWAYS POINTED OUT (AND EMPHASIZED AS FACT) IS THAT SHE WAS "FEARSOME," "AMBITIOUS," "RUTHLESS"...

COMMON (AND VALUED) CHARACTER TRAITS IN JUST ABOUT EVERY EMPEROR IN HISTORY...

...but clearly not as easy to digest in an empress.

TEMPLE GRANDIN

ANIMAL WHISPERER

ON AUGUST 29, IN BOSTON, A BABY UNLIKE ANY OTHER IS BORN: MARY TEMPLE GRANDIN.

SHE NEVER SMILES. SHE NEVER LAUGHS. SHE CRIES WHEN ANYONE TRIES TO PICK HER UP.

INSTEAD OF PLAYING WITH LEGOS, SHE PEES ON THE FLOOR.

INSTEAD OF PLAYING WITH CARDS, SHE EATS THEM.

FREQUENTLY, SHE SCREAMS, HITS HERSELF IN THE HEAD, AND SMASHES EVERYTHING IN HER PATH.

NOBODY CAN FIGURE OUT WHAT SHE'S THINKING.

...Or even *if* she's thinking!

Richard!! She's just *special*, that's all!

BUT BY THE AGE OF THREE, TEMPLE STILL ISN'T TALKING. SO HER MOTHER TAKES HER TO SEE A NEUROLOGIST.

THE DOCTOR ADMINISTERS A BATTERY OF TESTS AND CONCLUDES THAT SHE'S NEITHER CRAZY NOR STUPID. SHE'S CLOSED OFF FROM THE WORLD, AND THERE IS A NAME FOR HER CONDITION. "AUTISM," FROM THE GREEK ROOT "AUTO"...

...MEANING, "ONESELF."

WHICH WOULD EXPLAIN, AMONG OTHER THINGS, WHY THE LITTLE GIRL IS FRUSTRATED AT BEING UNABLE TO EXPRESS HERSELF AND CAN'T STAND PHYSICAL CONTACT DESPITE CRAVING AFFECTION.

She's *retarded*, basically!

likes to self-soothe between cushions

IN THESE DAYS, DOCTORS KNOW LITTLE ABOUT AUTISM. THEY BLAME IT ON DISTANT PARENTS WHO DON'T COMMUNICATE ENOUGH WITH THEIR BABY.

Normal brain

Degenerate brain

Grapefruit

OF COURSE, THIS IS COMPLETELY INACCURATE.

Thank you, Doctor.

TEMPLE'S BRAIN IS DEVELOPING VERY QUICKLY, BUT IN AN UNUSUAL WAY.

HER FATHER WANTS TO PLACE HER IN A PSYCHIATRIC HOSPITAL ASAP. BUT HER MOTHER SEES THINGS DIFFERENTLY.

You're not like others. But you're no less intelligent than others.

HER MOTHER SENDS HER TO A SPEECH THERAPIST THREE TIMES A WEEK. HE TEACHES HER TO IDENTIFY DIFFERENT SOUNDS, THEN TO FORM WORDS, AND THEN TO ASSOCIATE THEM WITH IDEAS.

eight?

infinity?

eye-glasses?

HE TEACHES HER TO FINALLY COMMUNICATE.

TEMPLE'S MOTHER SENSES SHE IS READY, AND DECIDES TO THROW HER IN THE DEEP END.

See you tonight baby!

TEMPLE LIKES HER SCHOOL, CLASSMATES, AND TEACHER. BUT LIFE IN THE REAL WORLD IS NOTHING BUT A SERIES OF AGGRESSIONS.

The bell hurts her eardrums.

Her tight collar is oppressive.

Her teacher's perfume makes her dizzy.

Her new socks are as itchy as sand paper.

She hears every single voice in the brouhaha of the cafeteria.

THE INFORMATION RECEIVED BY TEMPLE'S BRAIN IS AMPLIFIED, DISTORTED, AND UNMANAGEABLE. SHE PANICS AND CAN ONLY CALM DOWN BY CONCENTRATING ON REPETITIVE, SOOTHING THINGS.

HER MOM TALKS THE SCHOOL INTO LETTING HER JOIN THE SHOP CLASS, WHICH IS THEORETICALLY ONLY FOR BOYS.

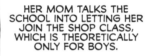

SHE TURNS OUT TO BE VERY GIFTED (PLUS, MAKING THINGS SEEMS TO RELAX HER).

HER VISUAL INTELLIGENCE IS FINALLY PUT TO GOOD USE. FOR TEMPLE DOESN'T THINK IN *WORDS*, BUT IN INCREDIBLY PRECISE AND DETAILED IMAGES THAT HER BRAIN FILES AWAY LIKE A SUPERCOMPUTER.

WHICH EXPLAINS WHY, FOR HER, ABSTRACT CONCEPTS SUCH AS EMOTIONS REMAIN A MYSTERY.

Mom! The baby's making weird noises!!

TO SUM THINGS UP: SHE DOESN'T GET JOKES BUT ALWAYS FINDS WALDO IN A MATTER OF SECONDS.

BUT TEMPLE IS ABOUT TO SUFFER THE MOST BRUTAL AND TRAUMATIC EXPERIENCE OF HER LIFE.

MIDDLE SCHOOL

FOR GIRLS

IT'S TOO BIG. TOO NOISY. TOO HECTIC. TOO COMPLICATED. TEMPLE REPEATS WORDS TO TRY TO CALM HERSELF DOWN. AND SINCE, ON TOP OF THAT, SHE HAS A HARD TIME READING FACIAL EXPRESSIONS OR SUBTEXT, SHE DOESN'T UNDERSTAND WHEN SHE'S BEING MOCKED.

By the way! We took a vote and from now on, your name is Bozo, 'kay?

hee hee hee hee hee hee

Temple Temple My name is Temple Temple Tem

SHE ROLLS AROUND ON THE FLOOR.

SHE SCREAMS.

SHE HITS.

SHE GETS HERSELF KICKED OUT OF SCHOOL.

HER DAD SEES AN OPPORTUNITY TO GET RID OF HER FOR GOOD.

She's a *dumb-dumb*, and you just refuse to face reality!

You will *not* talk about my daughter like that!!

1,000 Pieces

HER MOM HAS ONE LAST CARD UP HER SLEEVE...

...A *VERY* SPECIAL SCHOOL. IN THE MIDDLE OF THE WOODS. FOR ONLY THIRTY STUDENTS.

HAMPSHIRE COUNTRY SCHOOL

(INCIDENTALLY, HER PARENTS GET A DIVORCE.)

A SORT OF PROFESSOR XAVIER-TYPE ACADEMY, WHERE TEMPLE FINALLY MEETS PEOPLE LIKE HER.

You're not here because of your weaknesses, but thanks to your abilities. And the two are connected.

TEMPLE FEELS SAFE AMONG ALL THESE WEIRD TEENS THAT SOCIETY DOESN'T QUITE KNOW WHAT TO DO WITH. SHE MAKES FRIENDS (BUT FAILS TO REALLY GET WHAT ADOLESCENCE IS).

Boys? Well, I find them less interesting than other species, such as cats and dogs.

HER FRIENDS NICKNAME HER THE "ULTIMATE TOMBOY."

SHE DRAWS VERY WELL, ESPECIALLY HORSES (BUT NOT PORTRAITS, BECAUSE SHE CAN'T DO FACES). BUT SHE DOESN'T LIKE TO LEARN. HER TEACHERS WORRY ABOUT HER INABILITY TO CONCENTRATE AND HER FREQUENT PANIC ATTACKS IN CLASS.

feels like a hunted animal, constantly on alert

HER MOTHER THEN HAS AN IDEA (YET ANOTHER ONE!). SHE SENDS HER TO WORK ON AN AUNT'S RANCH...

...IN ARIZONA.

THIS IS A REVELATION FOR TEMPLE. SHE FEELS A VERY STRONG (AND STRANGE) EMPATHY FOR CATTLE. SHE'S NEVER FELT THAT CLOSE TO ANYONE ELSE BEFORE.

Hi there, gorgeous.

SHE NOTICES THE ANIMALS STAND STILL WHILE CONFINED IN THE SQUEEZE CHUTE PRIOR TO VACCINATION. THEY LOOK SO CALM AND PEACEFUL THAT IT MAKES HER WANT TO TRY IT (IN SECRET).

SHE FEELS COZY. ENVELOPED. SHE FEELS SOOO GOOD.

BACK AT SCHOOL, SHE MAKES A REPLICA FOR HERSELF, WHICH SHE CALLS THE "HUG MACHINE." SHE REGULARLY ASKS HER ROOMMATE TO PUT HER IN IT FOR AN HOUR.

Okaaay.

Thanks! See you later!

SHE HAS HER FRIENDS TRY IT AND OBSERVES, ANALYZES, AND STUDIES THEIR REACTIONS.

Would you say you feel relaxed?

Uuuumm... yes.

SHE GRADUALLY IMPROVES HER MACHINE.

SHE'S OBSESSED, AND SHE LOVES IT. SHE HAS FOUND HER CALLING. SHE WILL BE A *RESEARCHER*.

AND JUST LIKE THAT, SHE TAKES AN INTEREST IN HER CLASSES. SHE ENJOYS SOLVING PROBLEMS. SHE DECIDES TO GO TO COLLEGE TO STUDY ANIMAL SCIENCE.

SHE CHOOSES HER RESEARCH SUBJECT: THE WELL-BEING OF INDUSTRIAL FARM ANIMALS.

You mean cats and dogs?

No, no. Just *cattle*.

IN 1974, NOBODY HAS EVER IMAGINED THIS COULD BE OF ANY INTEREST WHATSOEVER. EVEN HER PROFESSOR THINKS IT'S POINTLESS.

Cattle? But...why worry about the well-being of animals that we raise just to *slaughter*?

NO MATTER: SHE GOES OFF TO DO HER FIELDWORK...

Take good care of the hug machine!

...IN THE MOST REMOTE RANCHES OF THE AMERICAN WEST.

SHE ISN'T EXACTLY WELCOME.

academic

doesn't laugh at the cowboys' jokes

from the East Coast

talks funny

and a **WOMAN**

WORST OF ALL, SHE'S DRIVEN BY A WHIM THEY FIND ABSURD (AND SHE'S POKING HER NOSE IN *THEIR* BUSINESS).

She talks about animals like they're *people!*

Nut job.

SHE IS HAZED MERCILESSLY. SHE FINDS HERSELF DRENCHED IN BLOOD A LA *CARRIE*, OR BOMBARDED WITH THE TESTICLES OF FRESHLY CASTRATED BULLS.

hah har hah

BUT TEMPLE ASSERTS HERSELF AND PATIENTLY PURSUES HER RESEARCH.

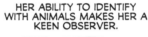

HER ABILITY TO IDENTIFY WITH ANIMALS MAKES HER A KEEN OBSERVER.

Come on, can't you see she's too *cramped* in there!!

TEMPLE KNOWS THAT, JUST LIKE WITH HER, A COW'S WORST ENEMY IS NOT PAIN BUT *FEAR*.

You yell and you hit to get them to move!

But the reason they won't move is because they're *terrified!!*

THERE ARE LOTS OF WAYS TO MAKE ANIMALS MORE COMFORTABLE, PROVIDED YOU WANT TO. TEMPLE PUTS HERSELF IN THEIR HOOVES (WHAT SHE CALLS THEIR "SHARED REALITY") TO UNDERSTAND WHAT IS CAUSING THEM STRESS. FOR EXAMPLE:

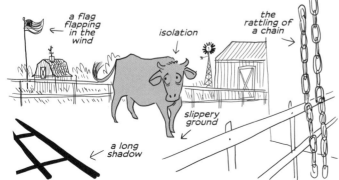

a flag flapping in the wind

isolation

the rattling of a chain

slippery ground

a long shadow

USING HER "ANIMAL SIXTH SENSE," SHE DREAMS UP WAYS TO COMFORT THEM.

We need to have them moved in groups...

and avoid straight lines...

SHE BEGINS TO DRAW EXTREMELY DETAILED BLUEPRINTS INTUITIVELY.

AS PART OF HER DOCTORATE STUDIES, SHE VISITS SLAUGHTERHOUSES WITH UNBEARABLY CRUEL CONDITIONS. SHE WRITES:

"If hell exists, then I'm in it."

SHE STARTS MAKING VIDEOS AND CALLS ON THE GENERAL PUBLIC TO GET THE LIVESTOCK INDUSTRY TO FACE UP TO ITS RESPONSIBILITIES.

Here!! I'm *giving* you my blueprints! Use them, for heaven's sake!

AT FIRST, PEOPLE THINK SHE'S CRAZY (OR FEEBLE-MINDED, OR BOTH). BUT TEMPLE IS USED TO THAT.

OF COURSE, IT'S DIFFICULT FOR A FRIEND OF ANIMALS TO WORK ALONGSIDE THOSE WHO RAISE THEM FOR SLAUGHTER. OF COURSE, IT WOULD BE EVEN BETTER IF THEY WEREN'T SLAUGHTERED AT ALL.

Unfortunately, the entire world isn't going to go vegetarian just like that. In the meantime, though...

Don't these animals at least deserve a better life?

Do they have to suffer just because they're going to die?

SHE WANTS TO ENFORCE STANDARDS. BUT HOW DO YOU QUANTIFY WELL-BEING? TEMPLE HAS ANOTHER WACKY IDEA: A SCORING SYSTEM BASED ON MOOS.

Because generally, if all is well, a cow won't moo. Or run. Or fall.

THE RATIO TO BE MAINTAINED IS THREE MOOS PER HUNDRED COWS.

INITIALLY, ONLY 25 PERCENT OF AMERICAN SLAUGHTERHOUSES PASS THE TEST. BUT TEMPLE'S INFLUENCE HAS BECOME SUCH THAT THEY ALL NEED TO EARN HER "STAMP OF APPROVAL." SO THEY HAVE NO CHOICE BUT TO GET TO WORK. ON TOP OF THAT, TEMPLE MAKES HER CRITERIA MORE STRINGENT EVERY YEAR.

FAST FOOD CHAINS, IN AN ATTEMPT TO IMPROVE THEIR IMAGE, DEMAND MEAT THAT MEETS HER STANDARDS.

SOON, OVER HALF OF ALL U.S. CHAINS ARE ON BOARD.

TODAY, TEMPLE IS A SCIENTIFIC EXPERT WHOSE WORK HAS BEEN TRANSLATED INTO TWENTY LANGUAGES. SHE CONTINUES TO ADVOCATE FOR FARM ANIMALS AND THEIR RIGHT TO BE TREATED LIKE SENTIENT BEINGS, NOT PROPERTY.

OF COURSE, SHE FEELS MORE COMFORTABLE AMONG ANIMALS THAN AMONG HER FELLOW HUMANS.

SHE GIVES LECTURES ALL OVER THE WORLD, BUT STILL MEMORIZES INNOCUOUS CONVERSATION TOPICS TO GET BY IN HER DAY-TO-DAY LIFE.

so um... er... great game last night, huh?

SHE STILL DETESTS INTRUSIVE NOISES, STRUGGLES TO UNDERSTAND IRONY, AND ALWAYS WASHES NEW SOCKS SEVERAL TIMES BEFORE PUTTING THEM ON.

And I still have my hug machine!

SHE GOT THE WHOLE WORLD TO LOOK AT AUTISM DIFFERENTLY, NOTABLY THROUGH HER BOOKS.

What really upsets me today is all those kids who are closed off, who don't think like others, and who aren't put on the right path: the one to Silicon Valley!

THIS FORM OF UNIQUE INTELLIGENCE IS ONE OF THE REASONS SOME PEOPLE BELIEVE THAT ANIMALS DON'T THINK.
BECAUSE THEY CAN'T EXPRESS JOY OR FEAR, ANIMALS MUST NOT BE ABLE TO FEEL THEM.

Kitty

THEY THINK IN SOUNDS, PLACES, SMELLS, MEMORY ASSOCIATIONS...

...KIND OF LIKE TEMPLE DOES. EXCEPT THAT TEMPLE LEARNED TO EXPRESS HERSELF WITH WORDS. SHE CAN COMMUNICATE AND SERVE AS THE LINK...

BETWEEN MEN AND ANIMALS, BETWEEN BIG BUSINESS AND ACTIVISTS. THE LINK BETWEEN BOTH WORLDS.

TEMPLE'S UNLIKE-ANY-OTHER BRAIN (SHE SEES HERSELF AS AN "ANTHROPOLOGIST ON MARS," AN EXPRESSION OLIVER SACKS BORROWED FROM HER) ENABLES HER TO UNDERSTAND LOTS OF STUFF THAT ESCAPES MOST PEOPLE.

THAT'S WHY SHE MAINTAINS THAT SHE WOULDN'T HAVE CHOSEN TO BE BORN DIFFERENT. NOT FOR ANYTHING IN THE WORLD.

My brain is not "broken." It is *what I am*.

SONITA ALIZADEH

RAPPER

SONITA IS BORN IN HERAT, AFGHANISTAN.

HER NAME MEANS "SPARROW."

SHE COMES FROM A VERY LARGE FAMILY IN WHICH GIRLS ARE CONSIDERED A FINANCIAL BURDEN.

HER FATHER IS MUCH OLDER THAN HER MOTHER, WHO WAS ONLY TWELVE WHEN THEY WERE MARRIED.

(She called him "uncle" at the time.)

SINCE WAR BROKE OUT IN 1979, WOMEN HAVE LOST MUCH OF THEIR FREEDOM. THE TALIBAN ARE NOW IN POWER, AND THEY ENFORCE THEIR OWN SEVERE INTERPRETATION OF SHARIA LAW.

SHE LOSES HER FATHER AT THE AGE OF NINE. SHORTLY AFTER, HER MOTHER ANNOUNCES SHE HAS FOUND SONITA A HUSBAND.

Huh?

ALTHOUGH THE LEGAL AGE IS SIXTEEN AND FORCED MARRIAGE IS FORBIDDEN IN ISLAM, MANY AFGHAN GIRLS ARE MARRIED OFF BY THEIR PARENTS AT A MUCH YOUNGER AGE.

SONITA IS THRILLED: SHE'LL GET A NICE DRESS.

SHE DOESN'T REALLY UNDERSTAND WHAT IS GOING ON, AND THINKS HER WEDDING IS "MAKE-BELIEVE."

SHE HAS NO IDEA WHAT REALLY AWAITS HER.

BUT IN THE END, THE MARRIAGE IS CALLED OFF AT THE LAST MINUTE.

AROUND THIS TIME, HER FAMILY DECIDES TO FLEE FROM THE TALIBAN IN AFGHANISTAN...

...AND HEAD FOR IRAN.

ON THEIR WAY THERE, THEY'RE STOPPED BY THE TALIBAN, WHO EXTORT MONEY FROM THEM BY THREATENING TO STEAL SONITA AWAY.

THIS LITTLE GIRL REALIZES SOMETHING FOR THE FIRST TIME:

SHE'S VIEWED AS MERCHANDISE.

HER MOTHER LEAVES HER WITH HER SISTER AND NIECE IN TEHRAN.

SHE ENDS UP IN A CENTER FOR CHILD REFUGEES, WHERE SHE LEARNS HOW TO WRITE (AND TAKES ANY HELP THEY CAN OFFER).

SONITA HAS NO ID AND NO STATUS SO SHE CAN'T FIND WORK. THE CENTER HIRES HER PART TIME.

ONE DAY, WHILE SHE'S CLEANING, SHE HEARS A NEW KIND OF MUSIC ON THE RADIO THAT HITS HER LIKE A SLAP IN THE FACE.

IT IS *RAP*.

SHE CAN'T UNDERSTAND THE LYRICS, BUT SHE'S FASCINATED BY THE RHYTHM, THE FLOW OF WORDS, AND THE *RAGE*.

IT PERFECTLY ECHOES ALL THE ANGER STUCK IN HER THROAT.

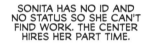

AT THE CENTER, SHE'S SURROUNDED BY OTHER GIRLS WHOSE PARENTS HAVE PROMISED THEM TO STRANGERS.

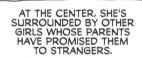

Lucky you! He's only twenty! With no kids!

He bought me for $3,000. How much are you worth?

THE INJUSTICE OF THEIR LIVES EATS AWAY AT HER, AND SHE STARTS WRITING.

Like all girls, I am caged. I am a sheep raised only for slaughter.

IT'S THE ONLY THING THAT BRINGS HER RELIEF.

SHE RECITES HER WORDS FOR HER FRIENDS.

Read the Koran again! It never said women are for sale!

SOME OF THE GIRLS ARE BRUISED. OTHERS BECOME PREGNANT, EVEN THOUGH THEY'RE STILL CHILDREN. OTHERS JUST DISAPPEAR.

Your words... That's exactly what I wish I could say to my dad...

SONITA HAS SO MUCH TO SAY. SHE WRITES EVERY TIME SHE HAS THE CHANCE.

Let me scream. I'm tired of the silence.

NOW SHE'S SURE OF IT: SHE WANTS TO BECOME A RAPPER.

SHE GOES TO SEE A PRODUCER.

I'm taking a big risk, you know: women aren't allowed to sing freely in Iran.

But okay.

SHE DREAMED OF A BIG RECORDING STUDIO AND LOTS OF INSTRUMENTATION. BUT JUST DOING HER DEMO MAKES HER FEEL PROUD.

Let me scream!

BUT ONE DAY, HER BROTHER BURSTS INTO HER ROOM: HE'S DECIDED TO TAKE HER BACK TO AFGHANISTAN AND MARRY HER OFF.

SHE'S SIXTEEN, AND HE WANTS TO SELL HER.

SHE CALLS HER MOM TO THE RESCUE.

SHE'S ON THE FIRST BUS TO TEHRAN. THEY HAVEN'T SEEN EACH OTHER IN YEARS.

BUT THE TEARFUL REUNION QUICKLY GIVES WAY TO THE REAL MOTIVE BEHIND HER MOTHER'S ARRIVAL:

...

?

SHE HAS COME TO GET HER.

Your brother needs $9,000 to buy himself a wife. And we're going to get that money by marrying you off.

What?? So... so *I'm* not as important?

⟨ANSWER: THAT IS CORRECT, SHE'S NOT AS IMPORTANT.⟩

You want to sell me.

You want to **sell** your daughter.

SONITA CAN'T BELIEVE IT: SHE HAS JUST FOUND HER CALLING AND DECIDED ON A FUTURE.

HER MOTHER JUST REPEATS THE SAME ANSWER, LIKE A ROBOT...

It's tradition. That's just the way it is.

SONITA THEN TELLS HER ABOUT HER LYRICS, HER MUSIC. SHE SAYS RAP IS THE ONLY THING THAT MATTERS TO HER.

That's inappropriate! If people in Herat knew that you sing, we'd be dishonored!

Learn how to cook instead!

AROUND THAT TIME AN IRANIAN FILMMAKER, ROKHSAREH GHAEM MAGHAMI, HEARS SONITA'S RAP.

SHE DECIDES TO FOLLOW HER AROUND ON CAMERA.

Go ahead, go ahead.

Just pretend I'm not here!

How about if you buy me, Rokhsareh? I am for sale, after all! Just until I do my songs. I'll pay you back afterward!

ROKHSAREH GIVES SONITA'S MOTHER $2,000. IN EXCHANGE, SHE RETURNS HOME AND GRANTS HER DAUGHTER A SIX-MONTH REPRIEVE.

Okay. Six months. It's go time.

WITH A BLACK SHEET, ROKHSAREH'S CAMERA, AND A LITTLE MAKEUP, SHE SHOOTS A VIDEO FOR HER SONG "BRIDES FOR SALE."

SHE PUTS IT ON YOUTUBE.

Send.

(THEN SHE TURNS HER PHONE OFF FOR TWO DAYS; THAT'S HOW SCARED SHE IS OF HER FAMILY'S REACTION.)

WITHIN TWO WEEKS, THE VIDEO IS SHARED, COMMENTED ON, SHARED AGAIN...

6,150

...AND THEN ONE DAY, SONITA IS CONTACTED BY AN ORGANIZATION CALLED STRONGHEART.

THEY OFFER TO SEND HER TO A PRIVATE SCHOOL IN THE U.S. WHERE SHE CAN STUDY AND WORK ON HER MUSIC.

We'll handle everything!

Thank you!

ALL SONITA NEEDS TO DO IS GO GET A PASSPORT...

...IN AFGHANISTAN.

BUT SHE DOESN'T HAVE A CHOICE. SHE LEAVES HER SISTER AND HER NIECE (WHICH IS HEARTBREAKING), AND HEADS FOR AFGHANISTAN.

Promise you'll come back!!

Of course I will!! What do you want from America?

SO THERE SHE IS, BACK IN THE LION'S DEN. BACK TO SQUARE ONE.

HERAT.

They'll try to stop me.

Fine.

I'll run away.

SHE'S REUNITED WITH HER FAMILY, FROM WHOM SHE NATURALLY KEEPS HER PROJECTS A SECRET.

DEADLY SILENCE

SO, um...

ahem

Did you like my video?

Yes. At least your head is covered.

Let Me Scream

(THE LITTLE ONES KNOW IT BY HEART.)

SURPRISE, SURPRISE, GETTING A VISA PROVES TO BE AN ADMINISTRATIVE NIGHTMARE FOR A YOUNG WOMAN TRAVELING ALONE. IRONICALLY, THE AUTHORITIES SUSPECT HUMAN TRAFFICKING.

Yes, I see! You're afraid people might try to **sell me**, is that it?

BUT BY A BIZARRE NETWORK OF CONNECTIONS FROM COUSIN TO BROTHER-IN-LAW TO AN AUNT'S NEIGHBOR, SONITA ENDS UP IN THE AMBASSADOR'S OFFICE

(where she improvises a rap song).

Let me out of this prison!

AND SHE GETS HER PAPERS.

SHE FLEES TO AMERICA WITHOUT SAYING A WORD TO HER MOTHER.

Flight crew, close the doors.

THE UTAH LANDSCAPE BEARS A STRONG RESEMBLANCE TO HER OWN COUNTRY.

SONITA

THIS IS SONITA'S FIRST TIME IN SCHOOL. SHE KNOWS HOW TO SAY THREE THINGS IN ENGLISH:

Hi.

Bye.

I am a rapper.

SHE FINALLY CALLS HER MOTHER TO TELL HER WHERE SHE IS, ALONG WITH A (TINY) WHITE LIE.

I'll be home in a year!

WASATCH

Jay-Z

HER MOTHER HANGS UP WHEN SHE HEARS THAT.

SHE PERFORMS HER FIRST SHOW IN FRONT OF A SOLD-OUT ROOM.

Hi. I am a rapper.

SHE SENDS THE MONEY SHE EARNS FROM IT TO HER MOTHER, WHICH SOFTENS HER UP A BIT.

SHE MAKES TONS OF FRIENDS, EVEN THOUGH SHE SOMETIMES FEELS OUT OF SYNC WITH THOSE OBLIVIOUS TEENS AND THEIR SHELTERED UPBRINGING.

Are you going to finish that?

Nah, go ahead and throw it out, thanks.

SHE MAKES DIZZYING PROGRESS IN ENGLISH SO SHE CAN REACH MORE PEOPLE WITH HER LYRICS. SHE WRITES THINKING ABOUT THOSE ENDURING THE PLIGHT SHE JUST BARELY ESCAPED.

SHE KEEPS ON RAPPING (AND DREAMS OF WORKING WITH EMINEM—OR BEYONCÉ), BUT ALSO SHE WANTS TO STUDY LAW AND BECOME A WOMEN'S RIGHTS LAWYER.

At Harvard, no less.

AT EIGHTEEN, SHE'S INVITED EVERYWHERE TO SHARE HER TESTIMONY, AND *SONITA*, ROKHSAREH'S DOCUMENTARY, TRAVELS TO FESTIVALS AROUND THE WORLD.

SUNDANCE

Sonita

SHE MISSES HER FAMILY TERRIBLY. SHE FORGIVES HER MOTHER (WHO IS NOW VERY PROUD OF HER). HAVING BEEN MARRIED OFF TO A STRANGER HERSELF AT A YOUNG AGE, SHE WAS JUST PASSING ON WHAT SHE KNEW, UNABLE TO CONCEIVE THAT THERE COULD BE A DIFFERENT WAY FOR GIRLS, OR THAT THEY COULD ACTUALLY ACCOMPLISH SOMETHING.

HER MOTHER EVENTUALLY FINDS THE COURAGE TO DISAGREE WITH AN EXTREMELY WIDESPREAD TRADITION—60 TO 80 PERCENT OF AFGHAN WOMEN ARE IN FORCED MARRIAGES, ACCORDING TO THE UN.

But I managed to convince my family, so I'm sure I can convince a country!

TODAY, SONITA WORKS WITH THE MOVEMENT GIRLS NOT BRIDES AND INTENDS TO ONE DAY RAP IN AFGHANISTAN—WHERE SHE'S GOT HER WORK CUT OUT FOR HER.

Her niece, married off in the meantime.

Girls are very *strong*. But they need *support*. And for those who have nobody, well, *I'll* be there.

(My thanks goes out to Women Make Movies and to Sonita.)

163

CHERYL BRIDGES

ATHLETE

CHERYL IS BORN ON CHRISTMAS DAY.

HER PARENTS DIVORCE WHEN SHE'S STILL A BABY.

HER MOTHER REMARRIES WHEN SHE'S SEVEN. HER STEPFATHER IS NOT NICE AT ALL, AND ACTS AS IF SHE DOESN'T EXIST. SHE BECOMES INVISIBLE.

stepsister

no presents (and it's her birthday, to boot!)

BUT WHEN SHE HITS HER TEENS, HE SUDDENLY TAKES AN INTEREST IN CHERYL.

A LITTLE TOO MUCH.

WAY TOO MUCH.

SHE LIKED IT BETTER WHEN HE ACTED AS IF SHE DIDN'T EXIST.

SHE LIKED IT BETTER WHEN SHE WAS INVISIBLE.

169

ONE DAY, SHE HAPPENS UPON A MAGAZINE ARTICLE ABOUT A NEW TREND IN AUSTRALIA: *JOGGING*.

We're running for *no reason!*

THESE DAYS, NOBODY RUNS. ESPECIALLY NOT GIRLS, WHO ARE ENCOURAGED TO DO... WELL, "GIRLY SPORTS."

THESE SPORTS AREN'T FOR CHERYL.

Woo-hoo.

SO ONE NIGHT WHEN SHE ISN'T OVERLY EAGER TO GO HOME, AND THE RUNNING TRACK AT HER HIGH SCHOOL IS DESERTED, WITHOUT REALLY KNOWING WHY...

...CHERYL STARTS TO RUN.

ONE LAP AROUND. THEN ANOTHER. ALL ALONE. IN THE DARK.

IN SECRET.

HER FEET HURT. ACTUALLY, EVERYTHING HURTS. HER LUNGS ARE ON FIRE. BUT SOMETHING STRANGE IS TRIGGERED. SHE STARTS CONVERSING WITH HERSELF IN HER HEAD, ADDRESSING HER PROBLEMS ONE BY ONE AND CALMLY ANALYZING THE SITUATIONS SHE FEELS TRAPPED IN. AND THE KNOTS UNRAVEL, AS IF BY MAGIC.

SUDDENLY, EACH PROBLEM HAS A SOLUTION.

EVERYTHING SUDDENLY BECOMES *SURMOUNTABLE*.

IT'S HER SECRET. HER OWN PERSONAL MAGIC TRICK.

CHERYL SLIPS OUT TO GO RUNNING AT NIGHT WHENEVER SHE CAN. ONE OF HER TEACHERS HAPPENS UPON HER BY CHANCE.

I saw you last night. You run fast!

HE ENCOURAGES HER TO SIGN UP FOR TRACK.

Even though you're a girl!

FOR CHERYL, WHOSE PRIORITY IN LIFE IS TO BE AS INVISIBLE AND LOW-PROFILE AS POSSIBLE, THIS IS UNTHINKABLE.

BUT HE'S SO ENCOURAGING THAT SHE DECIDES TO GO FOR IT.

BUT THE SCHOOL IS AGAINST IT.

YOU SEE, GIRLS ARE NOT SUPPOSED TO RUN.

It can damage the reproductive system!

Uh...really? But how?

That's just the way it is.

Oh. Okay.

THE ISSUE IS PUT TO A VOTE AND CHERYL IS EVENTUALLY ALLOWED ON THE TRACK, PROVIDED SHE KEEPS AWAY FROM THE BOYS ON THE TEAM, AS SHE REPRESENTS A "DISTRACTION."

Oh. Okay.

BUT IT MATTERS NOT. AT EACH PRACTICE, SHE EXPERIENCES THAT AMAZING FEELING OF BEING IN CONTROL OF HER LIFE, OF BEING INVINCIBLE.

EVENTUALLY, EVERYBODY IS FORCED TO ADMIT IT:

CHERYL IS *VERY FAST*.

SO FAST THAT SHE FINDS HERSELF ENROLLED IN A RACE AT THE AMATEUR ATHLETIC UNION (AAU), WHICH ORGANIZES WOMEN'S COMPETITIONS.

Who, *me?!*

AND SO THERE CHERYL IS, AT THE STARTING LINE OF A TWO-AND-A-HALF MILE RACE.

What the heck am I doing here? I'm just a nobody!

ferocious imposter syndrome

SHE'S SCARED TO DEATH.
WHAT WAS SHE THINKING?
HER, CHERYL, THE
INSIGNIFICANT LITTLE
HIGH SCHOOL GIRL?
WHAT CAN SHE POSSIBLY
HOPE FOR AGAINST THESE
EXPERIENCED ATHLETES?

THE RACE STARTS. AND AS ALWAYS,
THE MAGIC TRICK WORKS.

Go ahead.
You don't care.
Run for yourself.

You don't give
a crap about
the others.

Let's go.

SHE COMES IN SEVENTH.
IN HER VERY FIRST RACE.
CHERYL, THE NOBODY.

SHE GOES HOME
AS IF NOTHING HAS
HAPPENED, WITH HER
WONDERFUL SECRET.

FROM THEN ON, NOTHING
IS IMPOSSIBLE.

SHE STARTS BY GETTING
OUT OF THE FAMILY HOME
AS SOON AS POSSIBLE.

I want
to go to
college.

Okay.

SHE'S THE FIRST GIRL
IN THE U.S. TO RECEIVE
A COLLEGE SPORTS
SCHOLARSHIP.

SHE SIGNS UP FOR RACES
WHERE SHE IS THE ONLY
GIRL. THE COACHES
UNDERESTIMATE HER,
AND MAKE HER START FIVE
SECONDS LATE SO SHE
DOESN'T GET IN THE WAY
OF THE BOYS.

No big
deal...

It's *even
more* fun
to beat
them
when I
start last!

HER STATUS AS AN OUTSIDER IS NOT ALWAYS APPRECIATED.

Try to understand, baby! The other guys make fun of me. They say you're a dude...

Get that hand off me.

SHE DISCOVERS THAT SHE LIKES LONG-DISTANCE RUNNING, NAMELY CROSS-COUNTRY, EVEN MORE.

AND SHE QUALIFIES FOR THE 1969 WORLD CHAMPIONSHIP (IN SCOTLAND).

BUT THE AAU DOESN'T COVER THE TRAVEL EXPENSES FOR WOMEN ATHLETES.

Have you thought about having a bake sale?

SO SHE PAYS FOR IT HERSELF. THE RACE TAKES PLACE IN THE MUD, ON HILLY TERRAIN, IN THE RAIN. THE WHOLE ENCHILADA.

BUT JUST LIKE BEFORE, CHERYL'S SPIRIT ESCAPES ELSEWHERE, LEAVING HER BODY ON AUTOPILOT, FREE OF PAIN.

CHERYL FINISHES FOURTH. IF SHE HAD ANY DOUBTS, IT'S TIME TO FACE THE FACTS.

Hey, wow...

Do I love to compete or what?!!!

SHE MARRIES A RUNNING COACH, AND THEY MOVE TO CALIFORNIA. IT'S ALWAYS SUNNY THERE, SO THEY TRAIN WITH HIS FRIENDS EVERY WEEKEND.

ALL THEY EVER TALK ABOUT IS THE MARATHON, NONSTOP.

I'm sick of hearing about your stupid marathon!

NATURALLY, SHE ENDS UP REGISTERING AS WELL.

AND SO SHE ENTERS THE 1971 CULVER CITY MARATHON.

26 miles.

26.2, actually.

That ain't nothing.

(still somehow feels a little like a nobody)

SHE TRIES TO DO WHAT SHE ALWAYS DOES, DESPITE THE PRESSURE.

Your race. In *your* head. At *your* own speed.

MIDWAY THROUGH THE RACE, AN "INCIDENT" DISTRACTS HER:

AN ANGRY RUNNER REFUSES TO LET A CHICK PASS HIM.

OUT OF MY WAY!!!

BUT *THIS* CHICK KNOWS HOW TO FIGHT BACK.

SHE FINISHES THE 26.2 MILES.

AND SETS A NEW WORLD RECORD:

CHERYL BECOMES THE FIRST WOMAN TO FINISH A MARATHON IN UNDER TWO HOURS AND FIFTY MINUTES.

THE FOLLOWING YEAR IS THE MUNICH OLYMPICS...

...WHICH CHERYL IS DYING TO TAKE PART IN, AS NOTHING CAN STOP HER NOW.

NOTHING, OF COURSE, EXCEPT FOR OLYMPIC REGULATIONS! WOMEN AREN'T ALLOWED TO RUN IN THEM (EXCEPT FOR THE 1,500 METER).

THE REASON GIVEN AT THE TIME IS THAT WOMEN AREN'T CAPABLE OF RUNNING LONG DISTANCE.

What is wrong with you people?!!!

IN 1981, CHERYL HAS A DAUGHTER, SHALANE.

SHALANE DEVELOPS A LOVE FOR SOCCER AT AN EARLY AGE. BUT IN HIGH SCHOOL, AS A BEGINNER, WITHOUT REALLY KNOWING WHY...

...SHE STARTS RUNNING.

IN 2008, SHE WINS THE BRONZE MEDAL FOR THE 10K RACE AT THE BEIJING OLYMPICS (WHICH HAD CHANGED THEIR RULES IN THE MEANTIME).

IF THERE'S ONE THING SHALANE HAS HEARD HER ENTIRE LIFE, IT IS:

Accept the fact that you are a lot more than you think you are!

AS WITH HER MOTHER AND COUNTLESS OTHER WOMEN BEFORE HER, RACING TAUGHT HER EVERYTHING SHE NEEDED:

- *To take control over her own life*

- *To not compare herself to others*

- *To realize that all challenges are within reach*

And all that without anybody's permission!

THÉRÈSE CLERC
UTOPIAN REALIST

1927-2016

THÉRÈSE IS BORN ON DECEMBER 9, 1927 INTO A VERY CONSERVATIVE, MIDDLE-CLASS CATHOLIC FAMILY FROM THE SUBURBS OF PARIS.

SHE HAS A HAPPY CHILDHOOD.

AS A CHILD, SHE WATCHES HER WORKING-CLASS NEIGHBORS ADOPT ORPHANS FROM THE SPANISH WAR...

And us, Mom?

...THEN, SEVERAL YEARS LATER, HIDE JEWS.

What about us? Still no?

THÉRÈSE GROWS UP DILIGENTLY FOLLOWING THE PARENTAL ROAD MAP LAID OUT FOR HER.

Be pretty and nice.

And a virgin!

THE FIRST MAN TO PROPOSE TO HER IS NAMED CLAUDE. THEY MOVE INTO A BIG APARTMENT HIS PARENTS PAY FOR.

THÉRÈSE IS A STAY-AT-HOME MOM WHO RAISES THEIR FOUR CHILDREN.

SHE DOESN'T QUESTION HER LIFE AT ALL.

BUT AT CHURCH, SHE MEETS MISSIONARIES WHO TELL HER ABOUT THE HORRORS OF THE ALGERIAN WAR, AND ABOUT MARXISM AND THE CLASS STRUGGLE.

You see, Thérèse? Man must free himself!

What about women?

THE CHURCH HAS NO ANSWER.

LUCKILY FOR THÉRÈSE, THE YEAR IS 1968,

AND SHE ISN'T THE ONLY ONE CALLING SOCIETY INTO QUESTION.

Don't trust anyone over 30!

The struggle goes on!

WITHOUT TELLING HER HUSBAND, SHE GOES TO MEETINGS AND PROTESTS WHEN THE KIDS ARE AT SCHOOL. SHE DISCOVERS PARALLEL WORLDS: ANTI-CAPITALISM AND FEMINISM.

What...what do you mean "*mine*"? What does that mean, exactly?

My body is mine!

SHE HEARS PEOPLE TALK ABOUT *PATRIARCHY*. EMANCIPATION. AND ABOUT *SEXUAL PLEASURE*, TOO.

What was that??

EVERYTHING IS NEW.

SHE ALSO LEARNS THAT A LEADING CAUSE OF MORTALITY AMONG FRENCH WOMEN IS BACK-ALLEY ABORTIONS PERFORMED WITH KNITTING NEEDLES.

WHAT SHE LEARNS, IN ESSENCE, IS THAT WOMEN ARE NOT FREE AT ALL. SHE JOINS THE MOVEMENT FOR THE LIBERATION OF ABORTION AND CONTRACEPTION (THE MLAC) AND EVEN FOUNDS HER OWN CHURCH FEMINIST GROUP.

If you really think about it, Jesus and Marx had the same ideals.

THÉRÈSE IS FORTY YEARS OLD. HER KIDS ARE A JOY, BUT HER MARRIAGE IS DISHEARTENING.

HER SPIRIT CRAVES REBELLION, AND HER BODY CRAVES FREEDOM.

WITHOUT LOOKING BACK, SHE GETS A DRIVER'S LICENSE, A JOB AS A CASHIER, AND A DIVORCE.

SHE TAKES HER KIDS AND MOVES INTO A TINY APARTMENT IN MONTREUIL, A NEW AND UNFAMILIAR CITY...

SIGN UP!

CGT

Don't berate me, I'll do it!

...BUT WHERE SHE FEELS AT HOME RIGHT AWAY.

SHE LEARNS HOW TO PERFORM ABORTIONS AND STARTS OFFERING THE SERVICE—IN HER OWN HOME.

Thérèse... I want an abortion.

Well don't whisper it! *Shout it out!*

MORE AWARE THAN EVER OF THE MORTAL DANGER FACING WOMEN, SHE JOINS THE FIGHT TO DECRIMINALIZE ABORTION (WHICH WILL HAPPEN A FEW YEARS LATER).

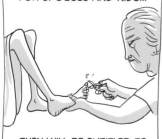

Simone Veil, minister of health →

We just need to listen to women!

HER HOME IS ALWAYS FILLED WITH NEIGHBORS, FRIENDS OF FRIENDS, AND ACTIVISTS.

Didn't your mom tell you to do your homework, buddy?

I'm on strike.

INTERACTING AND CONNECTING WITH THESE PEOPLE IS A SUBSTITUTE FOR THE COLLEGE EXPERIENCE THÉRÈSE NEVER HAD.

SHE'S NOW FULLY DEDICATED TO ACTIVISM, WHICH HELPS HER DEAL WITH PROBLEMS THROUGHOUT HER LIFE.

TWENTY YEARS LATER, FOR EXAMPLE, THÉRÈSE IS CARING FOR HER DYING MOTHER WHILE SHE HERSELF IS A SINGLE GRANDMOTHER (AND NOT EXACTLY ROLLING IN DOUGH).

Is the water warm enough, Mom?

IT'S A TRYING EXPERIENCE, AND SHE PROMISES HERSELF HER OWN KIDS WILL NEVER HAVE TO GO THROUGH IT.

ADULT DIAPERS

SHE STARTS FANTASIZING ABOUT THE PERFECT PLACE FOR SENIOR WOMEN, WHERE, AFTER A LIFETIME CARING FOR SPOUSES AND KIDS...

...THEY WILL BE ENTITLED TO PEACE, AUTONOMY, WELL-BEING, AND DIGNITY.

A PLACE TO LIVE FREE FROM THE JUDGEMENT OF A SOCIETY THAT CONSIDERS THEM TO BE...

A: A BURDEN
B: A MONEY-MAKING TARGET FOR CRUISE SHIP COMPANIES
C: ALL OF THE ABOVE

'Night, Mom.

THÉRÈSE CONSIDERS THIS TIME OF HER LIFE AS THE "GOLDEN YEARS," AND SHE SHARES IT WITH HER NEW LOVER.

If only in just the sexual sense! Finally! Passion without the pressure of performance!

AT FIRST, NOBODY BELIEVES IN HER UTOPIAN PROJECT. NOBODY WANTS TO FUND A HOME FOR OLD LADIES (NAMELY BECAUSE, BY DEFINITION, IT WOULD BE RESERVED EXCLUSIVELY FOR WOMEN).

But... they're the ones who need it the most!

Elderly women are statistically more isolated and poorer than men!*

(*40% less income)

THE DEVASTATING EFFECTS OF THE 2003 HEAT WAVE PUT PRESSURE ON THE POLITICIANS, WHO EVENTUALLY FORK OUT THE MONEY.

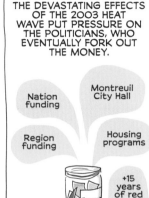

Nation funding

Montreuil City Hall

Region funding

Housing programs

THANKS!

+15 years of red tape for Thérèse

THE CITY OF MONTREUIL PROVIDES A PLOT OF LAND, WHERE CONSTRUCTION BEGINS ON...

The Home for Baba Yagas

BABA YAGAS ARE NICE OLD LADIES FROM RUSSIAN FOLKLORE WHO LIVE IN GINGERBREAD HOUSES AND TELL STORIES TO CHILDREN...

...BUT THEY DEVOUR THE CHILDREN THAT MUNCH ON THEIR HOUSES.

THE HOME FOR BABA YAGAS, WHICH FINALLY OPENS ITS DOORS THANKS TO THÉRÈSE, MONIQUE BRAGARD, AND SUZANNE GOUEFFIC, IS AN "ANTI-RETIREMENT HOME."

IT'S A RESIDENCE RUN BY ELDERLY WOMEN WITH MODEST MEANS, WHERE EVERYBODY HAS THEIR OWN SPACE (BUT NO GINGERBREAD WALLS).

NO NURSING STAFF, NO HOSPITAL ROOMS, BUT INSTEAD ABOUT TWENTY SMALL, PRIVATE, LOW-RENT APARTMENTS AS WELL AS COMMUNITY AREAS.

EACH RESIDENT HAS TO DONATE TEN HOURS OF HER TIME PER WEEK, AND EXPENSES ARE SHARED.

I don't believe it! We're out of Fig Newtons already!

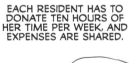

NO, OLD AGE IS NOT A DISASTER

THERE ARE SIX PRINCIPLES THE BABA YAGAS LIVE BY:

COMMUNITY SERVICE, SELF-MANAGEMENT, SECULARISM, ENVIRONMENTALISM, SOLIDARITY, AND FEMINISM (OF COURSE).

THE IDEA IS TO POSTPONE AS LONG AS POSSIBLE (OR EVEN AVOID) MOVING INTO A NURSING HOME (AND TO MORE OR LESS MANAGE ON YOUR OWN, DEPENDING ON EACH WOMAN'S CAPABILITIES).

And for that, you need to stay alert, useful, and happy!

WHICH IS WHY, UNLIKE A TYPICAL RETIREMENT HOME...

...Marie-Christine, you've just won a thirty-volume set of the Encyclopedia Britannica!

...THE BABA YAGAS ORGANIZE LECTURES, DISCUSSIONS, CULTURAL OUTINGS, NEIGHBORHOOD LUNCHES...

...AS WELL AS LOW-INTENSITY AEROBICS, ERGOTHERAPY, DRAWING WORKSHOPS WITH LIVE MODELS...

...AND EVEN "THE UNIVERSITY OF KNOWLEDGE FOR OLD FOLKS": A FUN PROGRAM OF CONVERSATIONS AND DEBATES WITH EXPERTS, PHILOSOPHERS, ETC.

Are there any questions?

THE ONLY CRITERIA FOR ADMISSION INTO THE BABA YAGA HOUSE, BESIDES LOW INCOME, IS AN AGE OF SIXTY-FIVE+ AND EXPERIENCE WITH ACTIVISM OR COMMUNITY WORK.

AND, OF COURSE, THE DESIRE TO GROW OLD IN A DIFFERENT WAY, AND *TOGETHER*. EVEN THOUGH, AS THÉRÈSE ALWAYS SAYS:

It's not always easy living with old ladies!

SO, FOR A CHANGE OF SCENERY, EVERY THREE MONTHS THE BABA YAGAS GO ON A TRIP.

THEIR MOTTO IS "AGING IS FINE, BUT AGING WELL IS BETTER." (That and, "Never go to bed angry.")

184

IN 2003, THÉRÈSE DECLINES TO RECEIVE THE LEGION OF HONOR. BUT SHE WILL EVENTUALLY ACCEPT THE AWARD IN 2008, IN THE PRESENCE OF SIMONE VEIL.

So that the legacy of women may be found elsewhere than in recipes!

BY 2020, SEVENTEEN MILLION FRENCH NATIONALS WILL BE OVER THE AGE OF SIXTY-FIVE. AND THEORETICALLY, WOMEN WILL STILL BE THE MOST AFFECTED BY FINANCIAL INSECURITY. THE GOAL OF THE BABA YAGAS IS THEREFORE TO *EXPAND*.

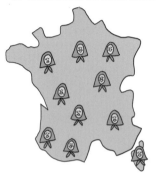

THÉRÈSE FIGHTS TO GET ATTENTION FROM THE POWERS THAT BE.

We are the largest electorate in France, I want us to be heard all the way in Brussels!

SHE ALSO VISITS HIGH SCHOOLS TO TELL YOUNG GIRLS THEIR BODIES ARE THEIR OWN.

So *choose* what you want to do with it!

(And get your diploma.)

NOW RENAMED AFTER ITS FOUNDER, THE THÉRÈSE CLERC WOMEN'S HOUSE OF MONTREUIL HAS WALLS COVERED WITH THE NAMES OF ILLUSTRIOUS WOMEN.

FRIDA   BARBARA

THÉRÈSE   SIMONE

THÉRÈSE REMAINS MADLY IN LOVE LIKE A TEENAGER UNTIL THE VERY END, AND IS FEATURED IN THE FILM *LES INVISIBLES* IN 2012.

(APPEARING NUDE FOR THE OCCASION.)

SHE DIES OF CANCER AT THE AGE OF EIGHTY-EIGHT, WHICH, ACCORDING TO HER WISHES, IS CAUSE FOR A BIG PARTY WITH FOOD, DRINK, AND DANCING.

For her, life was a struggle and a party!

UTOPIA WAS THE DRIVING FORCE FOR THÉRÈSE, WHO DIDN'T BELIEVE IN TRADITIONAL POLITICS.

IN HER MIND, ALL PROJECTS OF SOCIETAL REFORM SHOULD START WITH A DREAM.

IT WAS HER COMMITMENT AND ACTIVISM THAT CHANGED THE COURSE OF HER OWN LIFE: SHE WENT FROM A PASSIVE, SELF-INVOLVED YOUNG WOMAN TO AN IRREPRESSIBLE BEARER OF COLLECTIVE HOPES AND DREAMS.

"And what a beautiful journey it's been!"

Pénélope ⚹

BETTY DAVIS

SINGER-SONGWRITER

1945-

BETTY MABRY IS BORN ON JULY 26, 1945 IN NORTH CAROLINA, BEFORE HER FAMILY MOVES TO PENNSYLVANIA.

AS A CHILD, SHE LISTENS TO HER GRANDMOTHER'S RECORD COLLECTION UNTIL SHE WEARS THE ALBUMS OUT.

SHE EVEN WRITES SONGS HERSELF, WHICH SHE ORCHESTRATES VOCALLY.

Ba Da Dum

Wooo, bake the cake of luuuuv

Dum Dum

SHE SKIPS A GRADE, GRADUATES FROM HIGH SCHOOL AT FIFTEEN, AND TAKES OFF FOR NEW YORK...

...TO STUDY FASHION.

TO MAKE ENDS MEET, SHE WORKS AS A WAITRESS IN GREENWICH VILLAGE'S ICONIC BEAT GENERATION CAFÉS...

...AND AS A MODEL AT THE PRESTIGIOUS WILHELMINA AGENCY (WHERE SHE'S A HIT).

THOUGH SHE DOESN'T DO DRUGS AND DRINKS NOTHING BUT MILK, SHE GETS CAUGHT UP IN THE NEW YORK FRENZY OF FASHION AND MUSIC OF THE LATE 60S: SHE WANTS TO DO EVERYTHING AND SEE EVERYTHING.

SHE AND HER BFFS FORM A LITTLE CLIQUE: THE COSMIC GIRLS.

THEY LIVE FOR CONCERTS.

THEY'RE FRIENDS WITH THE GROUPIES, BUT THEIR APPROACH IS DIFFERENT: THEY ARE MORE FASCINATED BY THE MUSIC THAN BY THE MUSICIANS (WITH WHOM THEY DON'T REALLY SLEEP MUCH).

IN FACT, BETTY IS FRIENDS WITH MOST OF THE ROCK AND FUNK SCENE OF THE DAY.

THEY ARE ALL SURPRISED SHE WRITES SONGS.

You actually know a *lot* about music *for a girl!*

FOR THEM, GIRL = GROUPIE.

HER FRIENDS' ENCOURAGEMENT LEADS HER TO START WRITING SONGS FOR OTHERS. SONGS THAT *DO WELL*.

The Chambers Brothers UPTOWN

ONE DAY, SHE GOES TO A CONCERT JUST TO CHECK IT OUT.

Jazz is a drag, but I totally dig the trumpet player's shoes!

THAT TRUMPET PLAYER IS MILES DAVIS. CAPTIVATED BY BETTY'S PRESENCE, HE SENDS HIS ASSISTANT TO ASK HER OUT FOR A DRINK.

meh

Okay.

Sure, why not.

HE IS TWENTY YEARS OLDER THAN HER. IN BETTY'S VIEW, HE'S A DINOSAUR: HE PLAYS OLD PEOPLE'S MUSIC AND DRESSES LIKE AN OLD MAN. BUT THEY ARE MADLY IN LOVE.

A bow tie?

Seriously?

AND IN 1968, BETTY MABRY BECOMES BETTY DAVIS.

SHE'S HIS MUSE. EVERYTHING ABOUT HER FASCINATES HIM: HER FIRE, HER STYLE, HER TASTE IN MUSIC.

This album even features a song titled "Miss Mabry."

MILES GETS A MUCH-NEEDED KICK IN THE BUTT: SHE GIVES HIM A NEW LOOK, PULLS HIM AWAY FROM JAZZ, TAKES HIM TO ROCK CONCERTS...

...AND INTRODUCES HIM TO HER MUSICIAN FRIENDS.

Hey.

Miles, Jimi, Sly.

BETTY TRIGGERS MILES'S ARTISTIC REVOLUTION. IN HIS VIEW, THE MUSIC SHE LISTENS TO IS THE NEW SOUND OF THE BLACK PEOPLE.

The blues have been sold to the whites!

HE IS STEEPED IN THE SOUNDS OF ELECTRIC ROCK AND COMPOSES THE ALBUM *BITCHES BREW* (A TITLE BETTY CAME UP WITH), WHICH SELLS A HALF MILLION COPIES.

BUT AFTER ONE YEAR OF MARRIED LIFE, MILES IS EXHAUSTED BY HIS WIFE, WHOM HE JUST CAN'T MANAGE TO DOMESTICATE.

You're too young and too wild for these ol' bones of mine.

HE ACCUSES HER OF SHENANIGANS WITH JIMI HENDRIX. SHE SAYS HE HAS ANGER ISSUES.

SHE LEAVES HIM.

But this doesn't change what I told you: you've got *freaking talent, you hear me?*

SHE WRITES A SONG FOR THE COMMODORES THAT GETS THEM SIGNED ON THE MOTOWN LABEL.

It's all thanks to you, Betty!

ONCE AGAIN, SHE REMAINS IN THE SHADOWS.

BUT SHE IS STARTING TO QUESTION WHY SHE ALWAYS HIDES BEHIND SINGERS LIKE THAT.

I've got things to say, too.

I could make my *own* music.

WHEN MOTOWN GETS WIND OF THIS, THEY PROMPTLY OFFER TO SIGN HER (WHICH SHE REFUSES).

They wanted me to relinquish all rights! Ha!

ERIC CLAPTON INSISTS ON PRODUCING HER FIRST ALBUM.

I adore you, Eric, but you're...um, don't take this wrong way...too mainstream.

IN 1973, SHE MOVES TO SAN FRANCISCO.

New York? Been there, done that.

THERE, SHE HANGS OUT WITH THE CRÈME DE LA CRÈME OF THE MUSIC SCENE, AND SHE HITS THE RECORDING STUDIO.

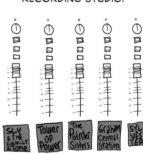

SLY & THE FAMILY STONE

Tower of Power

The Pointer Sisters

Graham Central Station

SYLVESTER

SHE FINALLY RECORDS HER OWN ALBUM AND HER OWN SONGS.

Just say when.

HER LYRICS ARE... PROVOCATIVE.

When I was his geisha...

Baby please, take me home...

Do you BLEEP them by the dozen?

I used to whip him with my turquoise chain

Oooooh begging me for more

I might not be here in the morning

I'm wiggling my BLEEP

Ride my broom, honey...

BETTY SINGS ABOUT SEX AND SENSUALITY. ABOUT HER DESIRES AND HER CONQUESTS.

Are... are you sure?

It's... unusual for a girl to let go like that, with such self-assurance...

How about a love song, instead? Huh, Betty?

Hey, good idea! I'll write a song I'll call "Anti Love Song"!

ON THE JACKET OF HER FIRST ALBUM, BETTY IS ALL CUTE AND SMILEY...

Betty Davis

...BUT THEN, UPON LISTENING TO IT, MAJOR SHOCKER: SHE MEOWS, SHE YOWLS, SHE ROARS, SHE SCREAMS.

It's like she's got one hand down my pants and the other one is slapping me!

SHE ISN'T EXACTLY SUBTLE ON STAGE, EITHER...

BUOYED BY THE SUCCESS OF HER FIRST ALBUM, BETTY DECIDES TO DO ANOTHER. BUT THIS TIME, SHE TAKES THE TRAINING WHEELS OFF AND SETS OUT TO WRITE, ARRANGE, AND PRODUCE IT HERSELF.

(AND SHE'S LIKELY THE ONLY WOMAN DOING THIS AT THE TIME.)

193

THE SECOND TIME AROUND, SHE'S EVEN MORE SURE OF THE ARTISTIC DIRECTION TO TAKE: SURROUNDED BY UNKNOWN MUSICIANS, SHE RECORDS THE ALBUM *THEY SAY I'M DIFFERENT*, WHICH IS EVEN MORE ACCOMPLISHED.

AS FOR THE LYRICS, NO MORE FILTER: SHE SINGS ABOUT HERSELF, ABOUT THE DIFFICULTIES BECOMING AN ADULT, ABOUT PROSTITUTION, AND KINKY SEX.

BUT THIS IS 1974. THE GENERAL PUBLIC IS RATHER UNCOMFORTABLE WITH SUCH EXPLOSIVE FEMININITY. BETTY'S SONGS ARE BANNED FROM THE RADIO AT THE REQUEST OF LISTENERS.

Hello! I'm calling to voice a complaint!!

HER CONCERTS ARE PUNCTUATED BY PROTESTS FROM RELIGIOUS GROUPS AND EVEN THE OCCASIONAL BOMB SCARE.

THE
ISIC
ES
THE VIC
NO

EVEN THE NAACP DITCHES HER.

She's a *disgrace* to Blacks!

HER LABEL DOESN'T QUITE KNOW WHAT TO DO WITH HER.

I dunno... Do songs that are more suitable for radio...

Less experimental... And quit singing about sex!!

THEY EVENTUALLY FREEZE HER OUT: SHE RECORDS ONE LAST ALBUM, WHICH THEY DON'T PROMOTE AT ALL. AND BETTY ISN'T EVEN REALLY MAKING MONEY ANYMORE.

It's not you personally! You're so talented! You're so *real*! And...

...and too black for rock, and too hard core for soul, I *get* it.

BUT TO BETTY, THE SLIGHTEST ARTISTIC COMPROMISE IS UNTHINKABLE, AND SO SHE OPTS TO DROP EVERYTHING, JUST LIKE THAT.

SHE QUITS MUSIC AND GOES BACK HOME TO HER PARENTS, IN PITTSBURGH...

...WHERE SHE'S BEEN LIVING LIKE A RECLUSE, ISOLATED, REFUSING ALL INTERVIEWS, SEVERING ALL CONTACT WITH THE MUSIC BUSINESS AND HER ARTIST FRIENDS, AND WITHOUT SO MUCH AS A TURNTABLE OR A CASSETTE TAPE AT HOME...

...FOR THE PAST THIRTY YEARS.

DURING HER SHORT-LIVED CAREER, BETTY LET HER SPONTANEITY AND HER INSTINCTUAL DESIRES BE HER GUIDE, NOT MARKETING AND SALES.

SHE MIXED MUSICAL GENRES, FREELY EXPLORED HER SEXUALITY, AND EMBRACED HER AFRICAN AMERICAN IDENTITY.

MOSTLY, THOUGH, SHE DID THE WHOLE THING *ALL BY HERSELF*,

FROM SONGWRITING TO PRODUCTION TO HER PERFORMANCES TO HER IMAGE AND ALL HER MUSICAL COLLABORATIONS.

EVERYTHING THEY KEPT HER FROM BEING BACK THEN...

...IS PRECISELY WHAT WOULD HAVE MADE HER A STAR TODAY.

SHE WAS SIMPLY AHEAD OF HER TIME IN EVERY WAY.

PRINCE TRIED DESPERATELY TO MEET HER (IN VAIN). AN INDIE LABEL RERELEASED HER DISCOGRAPHY. THE LIKES OF LENNY KRAVITZ, LUDACRIS, AND TALIB KWELI (AMONG OTHERS) HAVE DONE SAMPLING WITH HER TUNES...

...AND YET SHE NEVER COMES OUT OF HER SILENCE.

UNTIL RECENTLY, WHEN SHE AGREED TO APPEAR IN A DOCUMENTARY ENTITLED *NASTY GAL.*

IN IT, SHE REVEALS THAT THE ONLY MEMENTO FROM HER YOUTH THAT SHE'S RELIGIOUSLY HELD ONTO IS A COAT HER FRIEND JIMI HENDRIX GAVE HER.

ALSO, SHE'S STARTED WRITING SONGS AGAIN.

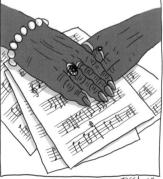

Pénélope

NELLIE BLY

JOURNALIST

1864 - 1922

ELIZABETH COCHRAN IS BORN ON MAY 5, 1864, IN COCHRANS MILLS, NEAR PITTSBURGH.

THE REASON HER VILLAGE BEARS HER LAST NAME IS SIMPLE: HER FATHER, MICHAEL COCHRAN, OWNS THE LOCAL MILL AND HALF THE LAND IN THE AREA.

Coochie coochie coo!

THIS IRISH IMMIGRANT WHO STARTED OUT WITH NOTHING NOW LECTURES HIS FIFTEEN (!) CHILDREN ON THE REWARDS OF A LIFE OF HARD WORK.

Yes, Daaaaddy.

ELIZABETH IS THE PRODUCT OF HER FATHER'S SECOND MARRIAGE. HER FAMILY NICKNAMES HER PINKY BECAUSE SHE ALWAYS DRESSES IN PINK.

BUT UNDERNEATH THAT CANDY-COLORED APPEARANCE LURKS THE MOST REBELLIOUS (AND STUBBORN) MEMBER OF THE ENTIRE COCHRAN BROOD.

HER FATHER DIES WHEN SHE'S SIX. HER BRANCH OF THE FAMILY TREE FINDS ITSELF EXPELLED AND PENNILESS.

Nighty night, children.

HER MOTHER HAS NO CHOICE BUT TO QUICKLY GET REMARRIED TO A MAN WITH THE MEANS TO CARE FOR HER FIVE CHILDREN.

TRAGICALLY, LUCK IS NOT ON HER SIDE. HE'S A DRUNK AND A WIFE-BEATER.

SHE EVENTUALLY RESOLVES TO ASK FOR A DIVORCE.

BUT THIS IS NO EASY FEAT AT THE TIME. TO WIN OVER THE COURT, HER DAUGHTER MUST TESTIFY.

Let's just say my stepfather has been drunk 24/7 ever since he married my mom.

IT'S BACK TO SQUARE ONE FOR THE WIDOW COCHRAN AND HER KIDS.

PINKY HAS TO WORK IF SHE WANTS TO HELP OUT HER MOM. AND THE NUMBER OF JOBS AVAILABLE TO YOUNG WOMEN IS FAIRLY LIMITED.

SO AT FIFTEEN, SHE ENROLLS IN A PROGRAM FOR SCHOOLTEACHERS.

AFTER JUST ONE SEMESTER, HOWEVER, SHE CAN NO LONGER AFFORD TUITION AND IS KICKED OUT.

Well how the *heck* are you supposed to manage when you're a girl?!!

ONE DAY, THE YOUNG WOMAN READS AN ARTICLE IN THE *PITTSBURGH DISPATCH* THAT PUTS HER (AS THINGS OFTEN DO) IN A STATE OF RAGE. IT IS TITLED "WHAT GIRLS ARE GOOD FOR."

Ha!!

Listen to this, Mom!

"A girl's place is at home, sewing and caring for the children. Otherwise, society would collapse. A woman who works is a *monstrosity*."

FURIOUS AND ON THE VERGE OF IMPLODING, PINKY GRABS A PEN AND CRANKS OUT A MURDEROUS RESPONSE TO THE EDITOR IN CHARGE OF THAT RAG.

Dear Sir,

Allow me to speak to you of a parallel world, in which women are forced to work to survive.

AMUSED, THE EDITOR-IN-CHIEF OF THE *DISPATCH* DECIDES NOT ONLY TO PUBLISH THE LETTER BUT ALSO TO CHALLENGE THE MYSTERIOUS "ANGRY LITTLE ORPHAN" TO COME SHOW HER FACE AT THE PAPER, IF SHE *DARES*.

HE OFFERS HER A JOB WRITING FOR HIM.

(BUT UNDER A DIFFERENT, MORE PROFESSIONAL NAME THAN PINKY.)

Hmm... let's see... Well there's that one song I like, "Nelly Bly."

(WHICH HE MISSPELLS.)

THIS IS FORTUITOUS, AS NELLIE HAS *LOADS* TO SAY TO PEOPLE WHO KNOW NOTHING ABOUT REAL LIFE.

HER EARLY ARTICLES FOCUS ON POOR WORKING WOMEN, ON THE DIFFICULTIES FACED BY WOMEN SEEKING A DIVORCE, AND ON THE WORKING CONDITIONS IN A PITTSBURGH FACTORY.

READERS GOBBLE UP THESE "BEHIND-THE-SCENES" ARTICLES. THE PAPER ASKS FOR MORE.

And I'm getting *paid*!

To *write*!!

BUT THE BIG MANUFACTURERS AREN'T TOO FOND OF ARTICLES ABOUT WORKERS BEING MISTREATED IN THEIR FACTORIES.

Get me the *Dispatch* on the phone*!!!*

Yes, sir.

THE OWNERS THREATEN TO WITHDRAW THEIR ADS FROM THE NEWSPAPER'S PAGES.

THE PAPER THEN OFFERS NELLIE A WONDERFUL OPPORTUNITY FOR A NEW DIRECTION: A "WOMEN'S" COLUMN.

Gardening, sewing patterns...

rage-o-meter

NELLIE WORKS HARD ON HER FIRST COLUMN, WHICH SHE HANDS IN ALONG WITH A PERSONAL NOTE

(A LETTER OF RESIGNATION).

SEEING AS SHE HAS (FINALLY) EARNED A BIT OF MONEY, SHE TAKES OFF TO MEXICO WITH HER MOM FOR A CHANGE OF SCENERY.

SHE KEEPS A TRAVEL JOURNAL (WHICH SHE SENDS TO THE PAPER IN SPITE OF HERSELF).

BUT SHE CAN'T RESIST THE URGE TO WRITE ABOUT MORE THAN JUST THE ENCHANTING LANDSCAPE.

Tuesday: President Porfirio Diaz had a journalist locked up in prison!!!

NELLIE'S MEXICAN VACATION IS CUT SHORT AFTER SIX MONTHS

AND SHE'S ESCORTED BACK TO THE BORDER.

DESPITE HER REPORTS FROM THE FIELD, WHEN SHE RETURNS, THE *DISPATCH* STILL CAN'T THINK OF ANYTHING BETTER TO GIVE HER THAN A VERY EXCITING GARDENING COLUMN.

SO SHE RISKS IT ALL TO TRY TO TALK *THE NEW YORK WORLD* (JOSEPH PULITZER'S OUTFIT) INTO GIVING HER A SHOT.

I'm not getting up from this chair until you agree to see me.

THE DIRECTOR, HALF IN THE HOPES OF DISCOURAGING HER, ASSIGNS HER A TEST ARTICLE ON A FUN TOPIC:

Mental asylums!

NELLIE GOES BACK HOME AND PRACTICES MAKING WEIRD FACES IN THE MIRROR ALL NIGHT. THEN SHE MAKES AN APPOINTMENT TO BE EXAMINED BY DOCTORS WHOSE DIAGNOSIS IS UNEQUIVOCAL:

Crazy as a loon!

SHE MANAGES TO GET HERSELF ADMITTED (WITH ALARMING EASE) AND THUS INFILTRATES THE NOTORIOUS WOMEN'S ASYLUM.

BLACKWELL'S ISLAND HOSPITAL
FOR THE MENTALLY UNHINGED

WHAT SHE DISCOVERS THERE IS INHUMAN CRUELTY: THE PATIENTS ARE INSULTED, BEATEN, TIED UP, UNDERNOURISHED, AND TORTURED.

HER ARTICLE MAKES HEADLINES ACROSS THE COUNTRY. IT'S A NATIONAL SCANDAL: THE AUTHORITIES LAUNCH A MAJOR INVESTIGATION THAT LEADS TO LAWSUITS AND THEN TO DRASTIC INCREASES IN THE BUDGETS OF PSYCHIATRIC HOSPITALS.

AS FOR NELLIE, SHE EARNS HER PLACE AT THE *WORLD*. AND AT TWENTY-THREE, SHE FINDS HER OWN PERSONAL BRAND:

INVESTIGATIVE REPORTING.

NELLIE'S ARTICLES HAVE TWO DISTINCT CHARACTERISTICS— THE SUBJECTS SHE ADAMANTLY CHOOSES: LOBBYISTS, LACK OF ACCESS TO HEALTH CARE FOR THE POOR, THE MISTREATMENT OF WOMEN PRISONERS...

...(BASICALLY ANYTHING THAT PISSES HER OFF)...

...AND, ABOVE ALL, THEIR *SOCIAL* ANGLE. NELLIE IS THE ONLY REPORTER IN THESE DAYS TO CHOOSE TO RELATE EVENTS BY JOINING RANKS WITH INMATES, THE POOR, STRIKERS, ETC.

ENOUGH!

HER NAME IS ENOUGH TO SELL PAPERS NOW. BUT SHE KNOWS SHE HAS TO CONSTANTLY OUTDO HERSELF TO KEEP HER PLACE, AND ONE DAY, SHE HAS A NEW IDEA FOR A CRAZY CHALLENGE.

Jules Vernes
Around the World 80 days

A trip around the world?! You can't be serious!! That would cost a fortune!! An escort for a single woman!! Plus all the luggage you'll insist on taking with you!!

BUT THEY UNDERESTIMATE NELLIE BLY.

I want to leave ASAP.

travels alone →

small Mary Poppins-type bag →

ON NOVEMBER 14, 1889, SHE SETS SAIL FROM NEW YORK ABOARD THE *AUGUST VICTORIA*.

SHE TRAVELS ACROSS ENGLAND, CEYLON, JAPAN, AND BEYOND ABOARD STEAMBOATS, TRAINS, AND HOT AIR BALLOONS...

SHE HAS A STOPOVER IN FRANCE, TOO, WHERE SHE CROSSES PATHS WITH JULES VERNE.

What I wrote was fiction. But you're actually doing it, Nellie! You're my Phileas Fogg!

THANKS TO THE MIRACLE OF THE TELEGRAPH, NELLIE KEEPS THE PRESS UP TO SPEED ON EACH STAGE OF HER ADVENTURE.

PEOPLE WHO HAD NEVER BOUGHT A NEWSPAPER BEFORE ARE NOW RUSHING TO NEWSSTANDS IN DROVES.

AND THE BETS ARE ON:

WILL NELLIE BLY MANAGE TO GO AROUND THE WORLD IN EIGHTY DAYS?

NOBODY WOULD HAVE GAMBLED ON HER, BUT NELLIE SETS FOOT BACK IN NEW YORK ON JANUARY 25, 1890. SHE GETS A BOOK DEAL OUT OF IT (AND EVEN A BOARD GAME).

JULES VERNE WARMLY CONGRATULATES HER IN HIS HOMETOWN NEWSPAPER.

"I never doubted the success of Nellie Bly. Hurrah! Hurrah!"

SADLY, HER BROTHER DIES AROUND THE SAME TIME. SHE DECIDES TO TAKE ON HIS WIDOW AND CHILDREN.

G'night!

SHE'S BACK TO BEING BROKE.

BUT JUST THEN, FATE INTRODUCES HER TO A RICH INDUSTRIALIST (FORTY YEARS HER SENIOR) WHO IS DYING TO MARRY HER.

Miss Bly! I have all your books!

IT'S AN OFFER SHE CAN'T PASS UP.

AND SO THEY GET MARRIED. BUT HE DIES SHORTLY THEREAFTER, AND NELLIE NOW HAS TO RUN HIS BUSINESS HERSELF.

THE FACTORY MANUFACTURES STEEL CONTAINERS.

SHE INVENTS A NEW MODEL FOR MILK CANS. SHE PATENTS IT, AND THE BUSINESS EXPERIENCES CONSIDERABLE GROWTH.

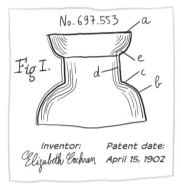

No. 697.553

Fig I.

a
e
d
c
b

Inventor: *Elizabeth Cochran*

Patent date: April 15, 1902

NELLIE TAKES THE OPPORTUNITY TO PROVIDE BETTER—AND UNHEARD OF, IN THESE DAYS—WORKING CONDITIONS FOR HER EMPLOYEES: HEALTH INSURANCE, GOOD SALARIES, AND EVEN A LIBRARY.

BUT WWI BREAKS OUT, AND THE JOURNALIST IN HER IS ITCHING TO GET BACK IN THE GAME.

Hello, *Evening Journal?* Hi, Nellie Bly speaking!

Do you already have someone reporting on the events from Europe?

SHE GOES TO AUSTRIA AND BECOMES THE FIRST FEMALE WAR CORRESPONDENT.

How do you feel?

SHE WRITES ABOUT LIFE ON THE FRONT FOR FIVE YEARS.

DURING HER YEARS IN EUROPE, SHE ALSO WRITES A LOT ABOUT THE WOMEN'S SUFFRAGE MOVEMENT THERE.

VOTES FOR WOMEN!

(AND SHE PREDICTS THAT AMERICAN WOMEN WILL SOON FOLLOW SUIT, TOO.)

SHE RETURNS TO NEW YORK IN 1920 AND CREATES A REGULAR COLUMN THAT DRAWS, AS ALWAYS, FROM HER ENDLESS SUPPLY OF PET PEEVES: CORRUPTION, THE BURDEN OF LABORERS, THE NEGLECT OF ORPHANS, AND OTHER INJUSTICES.

TAP TAP TAP TAP TAP TAP

BUT TWO YEARS LATER, SHE CONTRACTS PNEUMONIA AND DIES.

Nellie Bly

Elizabeth Cochran Seaman

By the New York Press Club in honor of a famous news reporter 1864-1922

SHE IS BURIED IN WOODLAWN CEMETERY, IN THE BRONX.

THE DAY AFTER SHE PASSES, *THE NEW YORK WORLD* PAYS TRIBUTE TO THIS WOMAN WHO PIONEERED INVESTIGATIVE REPORTING AND ANNOUNCES THE DEATH OF "THE BEST REPORTER IN AMERICA."

EVERY YEAR, THE NEW YORK PRESS CLUB AWARDS THE NELLIE BLY CUB REPORTER AWARD TO THE MOST OUTSTANDING YOUNG JOURNALIST.

Penélope*

THE SHAGGS

ROCK STARS

1948/49/51-

AUSTIN WIGGIN JR. IS A VERY SUPERSTITIOUS YOUNG MAN. HIS MOTHER OFTEN READS HIS PALMS.

SHE PREDICTS THREE THINGS FOR HIM:

- You'll marry a blonde.

- You'll have two sons.

- You'll also have girls who will become rock stars.

BUT AUSTIN DOESN'T EVEN PARTICULARLY LIKE MUSIC.

SURE ENOUGH, HE MARRIES A BLONDE, ANNIE, WHO DOESN'T PARTICULARLY LIKE MUSIC EITHER.

THEY DO INDEED HAVE TWO SONS, AND FOUR DAUGHTERS AS WELL, ALL BORN IN FREMONT, NEW HAMPSHIRE.

Dorothy (Dot)
↙ Betty
↙ Helen
↓ Rachel

FREMONT IS A BLEAK LITTLE TOWN THAT ALL MAJOR HIGHWAYS AVOID AND WHOSE RESIDENTS ALL SORT OF LOOK ALIKE.

AUSTIN WORKS IN A FACTORY THAT MAKES HANDKERCHIEFS, BUT LONGS TO SHINE IN FRONT OF HIS NEIGHBORS.

THEN HE REMEMBERS HIS MOTHER'S THIRD PROPHECY, AND ONE EVENING BEFORE DESSERT, HE ANNOUNCES TO HIS DAUGHTERS:

You're going to start a rock band.

THIS COMES AS A SURPRISE. NONE OF THEM PARTICULARLY LIKE MUSIC, AND THEIR FATHER HAS ALWAYS FORBIDDEN THEM FROM GOING TO CONCERTS.

HE BUYS THEM INSTRUMENTS AND ASSIGNS ONE TO EACH OF THE THREE OLDEST GIRLS.

THEN HE ORDERS THEM TO COMPOSE SOME SONGS.

DOT WRITES ABOUT WHAT SHE KNOWS: HALLOWEEN, HER CAT FOOT FOOT WHO HAD RUN AWAY, HER MOM AND DAD...

Lalalala
parents are wonderful
(has no idea what she's doing)

TO PUT THEM ON THE RIGHT TRACK, AUSTIN PROMPTLY SIGNS THEM UP FOR A TALENT SHOW. HIS GIRLS ARE WORRIED.

But, Dad, we don't know how to play!

HE WON'T HEAR IT.

HE BAPTIZES THEM THE SHAGGS, IN REFERENCE TO A HAIRSTYLE THAT'S POPULAR AT THE TIME. THEN HE MAKES THEM GET UP ON STAGE.

THE AUDIENCE ERUPTS INTO LAUGHTER. THEY'RE BOOED AND ALL MANNER OF PROJECTILES ARE LAUNCHED AT THEM.

THEIR DAD DRIVES THEM HOME, FURIOUS. BUT THE ADVERSITY ONLY RENEWS HIS DETERMINATION.

Let that be a lesson to you!! You're going to have to put in the time if you want to be famous!!

But we don't want to be famo— Shh.

NONE OF THE GIRLS DARE STAND UP TO THEIR FATHER.

AND TO "PUT IN THE TIME," HE COMES UP WITH A WHOLE REGIMEN.

FIRST, HE TAKES THE GIRLS OUT OF SCHOOL SO THEY CAN CONCENTRATE 100 PERCENT ON THEIR MUSIC.

THEY AREN'T THAT POPULAR TO BEGIN WITH, BUT THANKS TO CORRESPONDENCE CLASSES, THEY NOW HAVE NO SOCIAL LIFE WHATSOEVER.

HE FORBIDS THEM FROM DATING AND DISCOURAGES FRIENDSHIPS.

She doesn't have time!

THE DAILY SCHEDULE IS PRACTICALLY MILITANT:

-WAKE UP-

| morning | **REHEARSAL** |

-LUNCH-

| afternoon | **REHEARSAL** |

-DINNER-

| | **ONE HOUR OF PHYSICAL EXERCISE** |

-BEDTIME-

ESSENTIALLY, EXCEPT FOR CHURCH ON SUNDAY MORNINGS, DOT, BETTY, AND HELEN NEVER LEAVE THE GARAGE.

three, four.

THEY FANTASIZE ABOUT JUMPING INTO A CONVERTIBLE AND MAKING A BEELINE FOR SOMEWHERE AS FAR AWAY FROM HOME AS POSSIBLE.

It's my turn, Betty!

BUT THEIR FATHER, EVER THE AUTHORITARIAN, WORKS THEM EVEN HARDER.

AND THEY REALLY DO TRY THEIR HARDEST. THEY DESPERATELY ATTEMPT TO IMPROVE, TO MAKE THEIR FATHER HAPPY, AND TO MAKE HIS DREAM COME TRUE (SO THEY CAN BE LEFT ALONE).

dada mama dada-dada mama-mama

BUT THEY'RE GETTING NOWHERE AND AUSTIN'S FRUSTRATED. SO HE OPTS FOR A SHORTCUT.

You're going to record an album!

AND SO THE WHOLE FAMILY TAKES OFF FOR MASSACHUSETTS, WHERE AUSTIN HAS BOOKED A PROFESSIONAL RECORDING STUDIO.

Dad!

Please, Dad!

No!

We can't play!!

THE STUDIO TECHNICIANS, UPON HEARING THE GIRLS PLAY, FEEL INCREDIBLY GUILTY FOR CHARGING THESE POOR PEOPLE SIXTY DOLLARS AN HOUR.

FOOT FOOT, WHERE IS MY FOOT FOOT?

BUT AUSTIN LOOKS LIKE HE KNOWS WHAT HE'S DOING.

You messed up, girls. Again, from the chorus!

There's a *chorus*??

IT SOUNDS LIKE THEY ARE EACH PLAYING IN SEPARATE ROOMS, WHERE THEY CAN'T HEAR WHAT THE OTHER TWO ARE DOING. SOMETIMES, ON A FLUKE, THEY WILL ALL END UP ON THE SAME NOTE. BUT NOTHING IS IMPROVISED. THEY'RE VERY FOCUSED AND FOLLOWING A SPECIFIC APPROACH.

IT'S SIMPLY *THEIR* MUSIC.

THEY RECORD TWELVE TRACKS FOR AN ALBUM FEATURING A STRANGE, AWKWARD-LOOKING COVER PHOTO.

NONE OF THE SOUND ENGINEERS WISH TO BE CREDITED ON THE BACK OF *PHILOSOPHY OF THE WORLD*.

INSTEAD, AUSTIN (WHO NOW REFERS TO HIMSELF AS THE "OWNER OF THE BAND") WRITES UP A LITTLE INTRODUCTION.

THE SHAGGS ARE LUCKY NOT TO HAVE BEEN CORRUPTED BY ANY OUTSIDE INFLUENCE. THEIR MUSIC IS AUTHENTIC. THEY'RE PURE. WHAT ELSE COULD ANYONE ASK FOR?

THE SHAGGS LOVE YOU AND THEY LOVE PLAYING FOR YOU. THEY'RE DOING *WHAT THEY LOVE!*

AUSTIN BOMBARDS RADIO STATIONS WITH HIS ALBUM, BUT NONE OF THEM WANT IT.

What the...

Oh, so our music is "too rudimentary"?! Well I say it's *your brain* that's too rudimentary to hear it!! There are sounds only certain people can hear!

Dogs?

IN SHORT: HE ISN'T GIVING UP.

SINCE HE CAN'T GET SUPPORT FROM THE MEDIA, HE'LL GET IT FROM THE PUBLIC: HE BOOKS THE FREMONT COMMUNITY CENTER.

Oh, no!! *No...*

HE MAKES A DEAL FOR A WEEKLY SHOW: FOR YEARS, THE WIGGIN SISTERS WILL ENDURE THE TORTURE OF PERFORMING ON STAGE FOR THE WHOLE TOWN.

EACH AND EVERY TIME IS AN ORDEAL FOR THEM; THEIR SHOW BECOMES THE SATURDAY NIGHT RITUAL FOR YOUNG PEOPLE (WHO WERE IN THEIR CLASS) AND *THE* PLACE TO GO HAVE SOME LAUGHS (AND SMOKE).

AUSTIN IS IN THE ROOM EVERY TIME, TO SUPERVISE AND THEN GIVE THEM A DETAILED DEBRIEFING AT HOME.

He even has a badge made for himself.

HE'S THE ONLY WIGGIN NOT TO REALIZE THE SHAGGS ARE A LAUGHINGSTOCK.

THEY ENDURE IT ALL— THEY HAVE NO CHOICE BUT TO KEEP AT IT AND TRY TO IMPROVE.

It's Halloween

THEY VALIANTLY PLAY ON, YEAR AFTER YEAR, LEARNING HOW TO IGNORE THE CRITICISM.

THE MOST REBELLIOUS SISTER, HELEN, ACTUALLY MANAGES TO MEET A BOY AT THEIR CONCERTS, AND SHE SEES HIM ON THE SLY EVERY SATURDAY.

THEY EVEN GO AS FAR AS TO GET MARRIED. BUT A TERRIFIED HELEN KEEPS ON LIVING AT HOME, AS SHE DOESN'T HAVE THE NERVE TO TELL HER FATHER.

(HE EVENTUALLY FINDS OUT AND CHASES AFTER HIS SON-IN-LAW WITH A HUNTING RIFLE.)

THAT'S SORT OF THE LAST STRAW FOR THE WIGGIN SISTERS, WHO CONFESS (ONLY TO EACH OTHER, OF COURSE) THAT THEY HATE THEIR BAND, THEIR MUSIC, AND THEIR LIFE.

twenty-six years old

AND THEN SUDDENLY, AUSTIN HAS A HEART ATTACK.

HE DIES AT FORTY-SEVEN, SURROUNDED BY HIS CHILDREN, WHO WEREN'T ABLE TO MAKE HIS DREAM OF GREATNESS COME TRUE.

I'm so disappointed, children.

FOR THE YOUNG WOMEN, THIS MEANS LIBERATION. THEY HELD ON AND DID THEIR BEST FOR A DECADE, WASTING YEARS OF THEIR YOUTH ON IT.

BUT THAT IS OVER.

THEY PUT DOWN THEIR INSTRUMENTS, NEVER TO PICK THEM UP AGAIN. THEY MOVE OUT, GET WORK, MARRY, AND HAVE CHILDREN.

THE STORY COULD EASILY END HERE.

BUT YEARS LATER, AN INDIE LABEL HAS THE BRIGHT IDEA TO RERELEASE *PHILOSOPHY OF THE WORLD.*

What's the genre?

You'll... You'll see.

FREE JAZZ MISC.

ROCK

THIS TIME, THE PRESS IS INTRIGUED AND GOES FOR IT. BE IT IN A NEGATIVE WAY...

This has to be a *hoax*!! Studio musicians playing a joke! Look, you can tell it's dudes with wigs on!!

...OR A POSITIVE WAY.

It's hard to believe these sisters aren't on drugs.

But this album is a milestone in the history of rock.

DETROIT SUCKS

(Lester Bangs)

THE ALTERNATIVE ROCK SCENE CELEBRATES THEIR SPONTANEITY, THEIR GENUINE NAIVETÉ, AND THEIR RAW INNOCENCE.

They're better than the Beatles.

ROLLING STONE MAGAZINE PRAISES THEM AND CALLS THEM THE "COMEBACK OF THE YEAR."

Comeback? We never went anywhere!

Rolling Stone

TODAY, THE WIGGIN CHILDREN (MINUS HELEN, WHO DIED IN 2006) DON'T WANT ANYTHING TO DO WITH MUSIC, EXCEPT FOR DOT, WHO RELEASED A SOLO ALBUM IN 2013.

DOT WIGGIN BAND

READY! GET! GO!

Do people really like us or are they mocking us? Honestly, we couldn't care less. Okay, so we weren't the best. We did what we could with what we had. And we did it wholeheartedly.

KURT COBAIN ONCE SAID THAT THE SHAGGS, WITH THEIR PERFECTLY INTUITIVE MUSIC, WERE AMONG HIS GREATEST ARTISTIC INFLUENCES.

THE SHAGGS

AND DOT STILL RECEIVES FAN LETTERS FROM AROUND THE WORLD.

A COPY OF THE ORIGINAL *PHILOSOPHY OF THE WORLD* RECENTLY SOLD AT AUCTION FOR $5,000.

Now that's something nobody else in New Hampshire can brag about

Pénélope*

KATIA KRAFFT

VOLCANOLOGIST

1942-1991

CHARLES AND MADELEINE CONRAD, A FACTORY WORKER AND A SCHOOLTEACHER, LIVE IN GUEBWILLER-SOULTZ, IN ALSACE, FRANCE.

ON APRIL 17, 1942, THEY WELCOME A LITTLE GIRL, WHOM MADELEINE WANTS TO CALL KATIA.

Because I'm a big fan of Miss Schneider...*

*French screen legend Romy Schneider, who played a Russian schoolgirl who married Czar Alexander II in the 1959 film *Katia.*

BUT A GERMAN-SOUNDING NAME ISN'T THE BEST WAY TO START OUT LIFE IN 1942, SO THE CHILD IS OFFICIALLY REGISTERED AS CATHERINE.

But you'll still be little Katia to me.

KATIA IS HIGHLY INQUISITIVE, A DAREDEVIL, AND A BIT OF A TOMBOY.

MOOOOOM!

A LITTLE TOO MUCH, IF YOU ASK HER MOTHER, WHO DREAMS OF SEEING HER BECOME A SCHOOLTEACHER LIKE HERSELF. SO SHE SENDS HER TO CATHOLIC SCHOOL, HOPING THE NUNS WILL TAME HER.

THIS PRODUCES THE EXACT OPPOSITE EFFECT: THE GIRL LEAVES THERE FILLED WITH A STRONG AVERSION TO AUTHORITY AND IGNORANCE.

In the beginning, God created the heavens and the earth...

sigh

FOR KATIA HAS FAITH IN ONLY ONE RELIGION: SCIENCE.

IN HER TEENS, SHE ANNOUNCES TO HER PARENTS THAT SHE WILL EITHER BE A VOLCANOLOGIST OR WRITE CRIME NOVELS.

Those...those are *men's* jobs...why??

THEY AREN'T ALTOGETHER WON OVER.

NEVERTHELESS, FOR HER EIGHTEENTH BIRTHDAY, THEY AGREE TO PAY FOR A TRIP TO MOUNT ETNA.

SHE SPENDS THE WHOLE WEEK COLLECTING VOLCANIC ROCK— BEST VACATION EVER.

BACK IN ALSACE, SHE CAN'T SIT STILL. ONE DAY, HER FATHER ACTUALLY LEARNS SHE'S SNEAKING OUT EVERY NIGHT...

...TO PERFORM THE GLOBE OF DEATH MOTORCYCLE STUNT.

HER PARENTS MAKE HER A DEAL.

CHOOSE A *GIRL'S* MAJOR, THEN DO WHATEVER YOU WANT AFTERWARD.

OK.

SO KATIA PLAYS ALONG.

SHE BECOMES A MATH TEACHER.

THEN A NATURAL SCIENCES TEACHER.

THEN SHE GETS A DEGREE IN CHEMISTRY.

Okay! Okay! You win!! Go study your volcanoes!!

METHODICAL, PRAGMATIC, AND INCREDIBLY HARDWORKING, SHE LANDS HER FIRST INTERNSHIP AT THE NATIONAL CENTER FOR SCIENTIFIC RESEARCH.

AT THE AGE OF TWENTY, SHE RECEIVES THE VOCATION AWARD FROM THE HANDS OF PRIME MINISTER JACQUES CHABAN-DELMAS.

A female volcanologist! How about that!

ONE DAY, A SCHOOL BUDDY SAYS TO HER:

OMG, you're driving me *nuts*! I only know *one* other person as obsessed with volcanoes as you! You two should really meet!

KATIA AGREES TO THIS BLIND DATE WITH A VOLCANOLOGIST.

Katia?

Maurice?

HIS NAME'S MAURICE KRAFFT AND, LIKE HER, HE HAS A STRONG ALSATIAN ACCENT.

IN THESE DAYS, NOBODY IS INTO VOLCANOES. NEEDLESS TO SAY, KATIA AND MAURICE ARE ABSOLUTELY OVER THE MOON.

Sir, ma'am, we're closing.

Hello, Maurice? It's Katia... Did you get home all right? I'm calling because... You told me about a book on the Stromboli, and um I can't recall if...

THEY GET MARRIED IN 1970.

FOR THEIR HONEYMOON, THEY COLLECT SCORIA SAMPLES.

WHEN THEY RETURN, THE KRAFFTS TURN THEIR LITTLE HOME INTO A VERITABLE RESEARCH CENTER.

Careful with that coffee pot Maurice.

It's Hydrochloric acid.

THE DYNAMIC DUO GIVES THEIR VENTURE A NAME:

VULCAN

Maurice the Geologist!!

Katia the Geochemist!!

(BUT THEY ARE FLAT BROKE.)

THIS IS HOW IT WORKS:

Maurice!!!

There's an eruption in Iceland!!

Quick!!

To the Krafftcave!!

THEY GO BEGGING FOR MONEY FROM THE LOCAL COMMUNITY, FROM MUSEUMS, MAYBE EVEN THEIR PARENTS.

Vulcan
Five thousand dollars

(Katia is really good at reassuring elected officials, what with her girl genius look.)

One dilapidated car, one trailer, and boom: they're off on their mission.

THEY GET A FIRSTHAND VIEW OF THE ELDFELL ERUPTION IN ICELAND, WHICH COVERS AN ENTIRE VILLAGE IN VOLCANIC ASH.

THEY RETURN TO FRANCE TO TALK ABOUT THE DISASTER.

MEANWHILE, VOLCANOLOGIST HAROUN TAZIEFF (WHOM THEY BOTH ADMIRE) IS LAUGHING AT THE ICELANDERS' LACK OF DAMAGE CONTROL.

They're using gardening hoses!!!

THE KRAFFTS DECIDE TO RAISE MONEY BY ANY MEANS POSSIBLE.

Slag from Eldfell!!!

50F 40 25F

THEY DONATE THE 12,000 FRANCS THEY RAISE TO ICELAND'S AMBASSADOR.

TAZIEFF IS ANNOYED BY THESE TWO KIDS AND THEIR CONTAGIOUS ENTHUSIASM, WHO ARE STEALING HIS PLACE IN THE LIMELIGHT.

The idol of my youth.

So disappointing.

(THEREAFTER, HE NEVER MISSES AN OPPORTUNITY TO PUT THEM DOWN.)

FROM THEN ON, THE KRAFFT SCHEDULE IS SPLIT INTO THREE PARTS:

- *Look for funding.*

- *Take off on spontaneous trips to "chase" eruptions all over the world.*

- *Come home and show the fruits of their research to the public.*

THEY SPEAK TO EACH OTHER IN INDONESIAN WHEN THEY DON'T WANT ANYONE TO UNDERSTAND, AND THEY MAKE SURE THEY ALWAYS HAVE ALSATIAN LIVER SAUSAGE ON HAND FOR BREAKFAST, REGARDLESS OF WHERE THEY ARE

(even when they must lick the morning dew off their tent, the only water source available).

DRAWN TO EXTREME CONDITIONS, THEY KEEP THEIR COOL IN THE FACE OF DEATH AND APPROACH CRATERS WITH RESPECT AND EXHILARATION.

THE KRAFFTS ARE PERFECTLY IN SYNC.

KATIA IS LIVING OUT HER CHILDHOOD DREAM WITH THE ONE PERSON IN THE WORLD CAPABLE OF SHARING IT.

MAURICE TAKES NOTES. KATIA TAKES PHOTOS AND COLLECTS SAMPLES.

SHE'S IN HER ELEMENT IN THE FIELD. BUT BACK AT HEADQUARTERS, THE OTHER PART OF THE WORK IS A DRAG FOR HER.

LIVING ON VOLCANOES HAS MADE HER EVEN WILDER, AND SOCIAL EVENTS (THOUGH A NECESSARY EVIL) BORE HER TO TEARS.

Let us toast to your generous contribution, dear friend!

BEING THE RESERVED TYPE HERSELF, SHE LEAVES IT UP TO MAURICE TO CHARM PEOPLE OUT OF THEIR MONEY.

SHE DOES INSIST, HOWEVER, ON ANSWERING ALL THE FAN MAIL FROM CHILDREN HERSELF, AS SHE'S A FIRM BELIEVER IN PASSING ON KNOWLEDGE.

Dear Mrs. Krafft,

ROCKS, PHOTOS, VIDEOS... KATIA OWNS ONE OF THE WORLD'S LARGEST VOLCANIC COLLECTIONS, AND SHE WANTS TO MAKE IT PUBLIC.

SHE GIVES LECTURES, PRODUCES DOCUMENTARIES, AND LAUNCHES "THE VOLCANO HOUSE" A FEW MILES FROM THE PITON DE LA FOURNAISE, A VOLCANO OFF THE COAST OF MADAGASCAR.

MORE THAN ANYTHING, SHE KEEPS CALLING INTO QUESTION THE ETHICS OF HER FIELD: DESPITE INCREASED KNOWLEDGE ABOUT VOLCANOES, LITTLE IS BEING DONE TO LIMIT THEIR DANGERS.

IN 1985, WHEN THE NEVADO DEL RUIZ ERUPTS IN COLOMBIA, OVER 23,000 PEOPLE DIE WHO COULD HAVE BEEN SPARED. KATIA IS LIVID.

SHE DECIDES TO REFOCUS HER APPROACH IN THIS DIRECTION AND MAKES EDUCATIONAL FILMS ABOUT THE DANGERS OF VOLCANIC ERUPTIONS FOR AT-RISK POPULATIONS.

THESE UNESCO-SPONSORED FILMS HELP SAVE THOUSANDS OF LIVES.

OVER THE COURSE OF THEIR CAREERS, KATIA AND HER HUSBAND NEVER MISS AN ERUPTION (EXCEPT FOR THAT ONE VOLCANO IN THE USSR THAT IS OFF-LIMITS). THEY SEE 175 IN ALL, AND THEY ALWAYS GET AS CLOSE AS POSSIBLE.

HAROUN TAZIEFF ONCE SAID THAT GOOD ADVENTURERS DIE IN BED WHILE THE OTHERS ONLY GET WHAT THEY DESERVE.

Well, I'd much rather be one of the bad ones, then.

ON JUNE 3, 1991, THE KRAFFTS ARE SWEPT AWAY BY A LAVA FLOW THEY ARE DETERMINED TO FILM FROM UP CLOSE, ON MOUNT UNZEN, JAPAN.

PERFECTLY AWARE OF THE DANGER, THE "VOLCANO DEVILS" (AS THEY'RE KNOWN) HAD PREVIOUSLY CLAIMED TO BE READY TO DIE AT ANY MOMENT. THEY WERE AWARE OF THE RISK, BUT IT WAS WORTH IT.

Twenty-three years spent checking out volcanoes, can you believe it?

KATIA WAS RESPONSIBLE FOR A LARGE PART OF THE DOCUMENTATION NOW AVAILABLE TO THE SCIENTIFIC COMMUNITY.

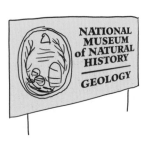

NATIONAL MUSEUM of NATURAL HISTORY

GEOLOGY

LIKE THAT OF A VOLCANO-HOPPING JACQUES COUSTEAU, HER WORK HAS INSPIRED PEOPLE AROUND THE WORLD TO FOLLOW IN HER FOOTSTEPS.

AND NOBODY WILL EVER AGAIN SAY THAT VOLCANOLOGY IS A MAN'S PROFESSION.

Pénélope*

JESSELYN RADACK
LAWYER

1970-

JESSELYN ALICIA RADACK IS BORN ON DECEMBER 12, 1970, NEAR WASHINGTON, D.C.

SHE GRADUATES FROM BROWN AT TWENTY-TWO, WITH A DOUBLE MAJOR IN AMERICAN CIVILIZATION AND POLITICAL SCIENCE (AND THEN SOME).

SHE ADDS A LAW DEGREE FROM YALE TO THE MIX.

Might as well.

While I'm at it.

SHE DREAMS OF WORKING FOR THE U.S. DEPARTMENT OF JUSTICE (DOJ), WHERE SHE WOULD BE SURE TO BE ON THE "RIGHT SIDE."

IN 1995, SHE MANAGES TO DO JUST THAT. FOUR YEARS LATER, SHE JOINS THE DOJ'S NEWLY CREATED PROFESSIONAL RESPONSIBILITY ADVISORY OFFICE.

You...you mean...

...Justice at the Department of Justice?

THIS IS BASICALLY HER ULTIMATE DREAM JOB.

AND THEN, ON A SEPTEMBER MORNING IN 2001, AMERICA CHANGES FOREVER.

WITHIN A FEW WEEKS, JUSTICE BECOMES TOUGHER; NO MORE HALF-MEASURES OR GRAY AREAS.

"Either you're with us or you're with the terrorists."

ONE DAY JESSELYN IS CONTACTED BY THE COUNTERTERRORISM DEPARTMENT.

(The name of the prosecutor on the phone is John DePue.)

232

HE HAS A BIT OF A DILEMMA AND NEEDS HER ADVICE: THE FBI HAS JUST CAPTURED AN AMERICAN IN AFGHANISTAN WHO HAS BEEN FIGHTING ALONGSIDE THE TALIBAN.

His name is John Walker Lindh...

Is it okay to interrogate him without his lawyer present?

Um, well...

...of course not.

BUT THREE DAYS LATER, THE SAME PROSECUTOR CALLS HER BACK TO SAY THIS:

Okay. Well, we ended up interrogating him anyway.

Now what do we do?

JESSELYN KNOWS WHAT THEY HAVE DONE IS ILLEGAL, SO SHE RECOMMENDS THAT THE STATEMENT BE SEALED IMMEDIATELY AND *ONLY* USED TO OBTAIN INFO ON AL-QAEDA.

But *never* against Lindh himself, you hear?!

BUT THE U.S. ATTORNEY GENERAL STARTS GIVING PRESS CONFERENCES WITH GREAT FANFARE, ANNOUNCING THEY HAVE A TERRORIST AND THAT HE'S GOING TO TRIAL.

MEDIA OUTLETS SHOW NONSTOP COVERAGE OF THE "AMERICAN TALIBAN."

HANDCUFFED, NAKED, AND WITH A BULLET IN HIS LEG, IT'S SAFE TO ASSUME THEY HAD NOT GONE EASY ON HIM DURING QUESTIONING.

His rights were respected to the letter.

He didn't retain counsel.

sick to her stomach

HIS CONFESSION WAS OBTAINED UNDER TORTURE: THE U.S. IS IN A STATE OF GENERAL HYSTERIA OVER THE FIRST POST-9/11 TERRORIST...

...AND THE BUSH ADMINISTRATION INTENDS TO MAKE AN EXAMPLE OUT OF HIM.

JESSELYN IS SHAKEN TO THE CORE: HER FAITH IN THE JUSTICE SYSTEM IS DEALT A NASTY BLOW.

But...but they're *lying*...

THE FOLLOWING MORNING, SHE REPORTS THAT FACT TO HER BOSS, WHOSE RESPONSE IS CRYSTAL CLEAR.

Forget about the whole thing. *Immediately.*

THEN JESSELYN RECEIVES A MESSAGE FROM THE LEAD PROSECUTOR ON THE LINDH CASE, WHO ASKS HER TO CONFIRM SHE SENT TWO E-MAILS REGARDING THAT FILE.

TWO?? I sent over ten of them!!

EXCEPT THAT THE E-MAILS (IN WHICH SHE WARNS THE FBI ABOUT THE ILLEGAL NATURE OF THE INTERROGATION) HAVE VANISHED.

No results

SHE BEGINS TO REALIZE THEY'RE TRYING TO COVER UP THE WHOLE THING.

THAT *HER OWN PEOPLE* ARE TRYING TO COVER IT UP.

No. We are *not* sending someone to the electric chair just because I kept quiet.

SHE CALLS THE IT DEPARTMENT, WHICH MANAGES TO EXHUME FOURTEEN E-MAILS.

A-HA!! I knew it!!

SHE PRINTS THEM OUT, HANDS THEM TO HER BOSS (AFTER MAKING A COPY, SHOULD THEY MYSTERIOUSLY GO MISSING AGAIN)...

J. W. Lindh Interrogation

J. Radack

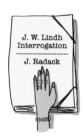

...THEN, DISHEARTENED, RESIGNS FROM HER ULTIMATE DREAM JOB.

SHE GETS HERSELF A JOB WITH A PRIVATE FIRM, BECOMES PREGNANT WITH HER THIRD CHILD, AND MOVES ON TO OTHER THINGS.

OR...SO SHE TRIES.

JESSELYN IS HAUNTED BY THAT INJUSTICE. UNSURPRISINGLY, THE DOJ NEVER FOLLOWS UP ON HER FILE.

TIME PASSES. SHE CAN'T STAND IT ANYMORE, AND DECIDES TO SEND THE E-MAILS TO *NEWSWEEK* (ASKING THEM TO KEEP HER NAME OUT OF IT).

THE MAGAZINE MAKES IT THEIR COVER STORY, IGNITING A NATIONAL SCANDAL IN THE PROCESS (AND THEY USE HER NAME).

ALL JESSELYN EVER WANTED WAS TO DO HER JOB WITH INTEGRITY.

Whew! I feel like a load's been lifted!

LITTLE DOES SHE KNOW, SHE HAS JUST LAUNCHED A HUGE WAR MACHINE AGAINST HERSELF.

FIRST, SHE'S TOLD SHE IS NOW THE SUBJECT OF A CRIMINAL INVESTIGATION (MEANING SHE COULD BE DISBARRED).

NATURALLY, THERE'S NO WAY OF KNOWING WHAT THE CHARGES ARE EXACTLY.

THEN HER NEW LAW FIRM STARTS RECEIVING CALLS FROM THE DOJ TELLING THEM THEY HAD JUST HIRED

"a criminal prone to stealing files."

SHE IS LAID OFF, OF COURSE (AND THUS, SOON TO BE BROKE).

RIGHT ABOUT THEN, SHE ALSO FINDS OUT SHE'S ON A NO-FLY LIST.

IT'S LIKE A BAD DREAM: THE SAME JESSELYN WHO COULD NEVER EVEN BRING HERSELF TO STEAL A PEN FROM A HOTEL ROOM IS BEING HARASSED BY INVESTIGATORS.

Tell us what you know immediately, or we'll get a search warrant!

THE DOJ CALLS HER A LIAR IN THE PRESS. A TRAITOR. A BAD AMERICAN.

BEYOND THE FACT THAT THESE ACCUSATIONS ARE SERIOUSLY JEOPARDIZING HER CHANCES OF FINDING A JOB ONE DAY, THIS IS THE WORST THING ANYONE COULD SAY ABOUT JESSELYN.

ew York Times

SHE'S UNDER TREMENDOUS STRESS (AND BROKE), WHICH CAUSES HER MULTIPLE SCLEROSIS (WHICH SHE HAS BEEN AFFLICTED WITH SINCE COLLEGE) TO FLARE UP.

THE SITUATION HAS REVERSED ITSELF INSIDIOUSLY: EVEN THOUGH SHE HAS DONE NOTHING WRONG, SHE HAS NO CHOICE BUT TO HIRE LAWYERS TO DEFEND HER (AND USE UP WHAT IS LEFT OF HER MONEY).

They've switched the issue around.

Now *I'm* the one under scrutiny. This way, there is no more talk about what I initially accused them of!

ONE DAY, SHE'S TOLD THEY'RE COMING TO ARREST HER AT HOME. IN FRONT OF HER NEIGHBORS AND HER KIDS.

JESSELYN HAS A MISCARRIAGE THAT NIGHT.

SHE KNOWS THE BUSH ADMINISTRATION WILL NEVER FORGIVE HER FOR TALKING AND THAT PEOPLE HAVE SET OUT TO DESTROY HER. TELLING THE TRUTH HAS MADE HER AN ENEMY OF THE STATE.

To those who scare peace-loving citizens with phantoms of lost liberty: your tactics only aid terrorists.

(John Ashcroft)

THIS TAKES THE CAKE, EVEN FOR JESSELYN, THE RESPECTABLE A-STUDENT WHO ONLY WANTED TO BE A PUBLIC SERVANT.

But if I'm a liar, what do they have to be afraid of? Why spend all that money and energy on trying to shut me up?!

THE CHARGES AGAINST HER ARE EVENTUALLY DROPPED.

I should hope so! What am I supposed to do, say thank you?

BUT SHE REALIZES THAT WHILE **SHE** DIDN'T STAND TRIAL, MANY FORMER STATE EMPLOYEES ARE BEING PROSECUTED FOR THE SAME REASON.

HER ANGER BEGINS TO TAKE OVER. SHE PROMISES HERSELF THAT FROM NOW ON, SHE WILL DEVOTE HER LIFE TO REPRESENTING WHISTLEBLOWERS (AND THAT SHE WILL NEVER AGAIN KEEP QUIET).

If they can do this much harm to an educated white American like me, I can only imagine what they're capable of inflicting on others in this country!

SHE REACHES OUT TO WHISTLEBLOWERS AND OFFERS HER HELP. SHE KNOWS THAT DISOBEYING (THEIR BOSS, THE GOVERNMENT) COULD COST THEM MORE THAN JUST THEIR CAREERS.

They'll try to destroy you.

Trust me.

SHE REPRESENTS MANY WHISTLEBLOWERS, FROM FORMER NSA AGENT THOMAS DRAKE TO JOHN KIRIAKOU (WHO DENOUNCED CIA TORTURE TECHNIQUES) TO EDWARD SNOWDEN.

SINCE THE GOVERNMENT IS TRYING TO SHUT THEM UP, SHE STIRS UP PUBLIC OPINION ON THEIR BEHALF AND GIVES INTERVIEW AFTER INTERVIEW.

This government is waging a *war* against our right to information!

NEWS JESSELYN RADACK
Lawyer
Snowden: Traitor or hero?

SHE FIGURES HER FIGHT IS ONLY JUST BEGINNING, FOR ON OBAMA'S WATCH, SEVEN WHISTLEBLOWERS ARE PROSECUTED (UNDER THE ESPIONAGE ACT OF 1917).

He's even worse than Bush!! *He* actually puts them in prison! To think I campaigned and voted for him!!

IN 2014, A DOCUMENTARY ENTITLED *SILENCED* COMES OUT, ABOUT HER ORDEAL (AND THAT OF OTHERS).

The notion that we have to choose between civil liberties and national security is a *disgrace*. A country that wants *democracy* must accept *transparency*!!

ALONG WITH FORMER PUBLIC SERVANTS, JOURNALISTS, AND WHISTLEBLOWERS, SHE LAUNCHES AN INFORMATION AND SOURCE PROTECTION PLATFORM.

EXPOSE FACTS

Whistleblowers Welcome

FEATURING HIGHLY ADVANCED ENCRYPTION TECHNOLOGY, *EXPOSEFACTS* ENCOURAGES WHISTLEBLOWERS TO SEND THEM THEIR FILES, WHICH ARE THEN SORTED THROUGH AND TRANSFERRED TO THE MEDIA THROUGH SECURE CHANNELS.

THEN IN LATE 2015, JESSELYN LAUNCHES *WHISPER* (THE WHISTLEBLOWER AND SOURCE PROTECTION PROGRAM), A RESOURCE THAT PROVIDES LEGAL ASSISTANCE AND ENCRYPTION SOLUTIONS TO WHISTLEBLOWERS.

WHISPER IS FUNDED BY DONATIONS AND AN ONLINE STORE.

BLOW MY BABY

FOR THE OVEREDUCATED YOUNG IDEALIST WHO DREAMED OF HEROICALLY SERVING HER COUNTRY, THE DISILLUSION SHE EXPERIENCED WAS SHATTERING.

But serving my country doesn't mean blindly following orders.

The real heroes protecting democracy are the whistleblowers.

And in the end, supporting them is my true ultimate dream job.

JESSELYN RADACK SAID THAT SEPTEMBER 11 LED TO THE WORST PERIOD OF HER LIFE...

...BUT THAT MORE IMPORTANTLY, IT WAS THE STARTING POINT OF HER CALLING AS AN ACTIVIST.

AND SHE SAID THAT NOW, SHE IS ALWAYS SURE OF BEING ON THE RIGHT SIDE.

Pénélope*

HEDY LAMARR
ACTRESS AND INVENTOR

1914-2000

HEDWIG KIESLER IS BORN ON NOVEMBER 9, 1914, IN VIENNA.

FROM DAY ONE, EVERYONE MARVELS AT HER BEAUTY.

HER PARENTS ARE JEWISH AND HALF-HUNGARIAN. EMIL IS A BANKER, AND TRUDE IS A PIANIST.

ALL DAY LONG, HEDY HEARS PEOPLE PRAISING HER LOOKS, BUT SHE'S BORED NONETHELESS.

AN ONLY CHILD, SHE TALKS TO HERSELF AND PUTS ON SHOWS FOR HER DOLLS.

HER FATHER EXPLAINS TO HER HOW STUFF WORKS.

HER MOTHER, WHO KNOWS HEDY WILL ALWAYS BE COMPLIMENTED, TRIES TO COUNTERBALANCE THAT BY BEING UNCOMPROMISING.

You can bat your eyelashes all you want, it won't get you out of washing behind your ears!

HEDY DOES IMPRESSIONS OF HER PARENTS, HER CAT, AND PASSERSBY.

Hedy!!

SHE LOVES MIMICKING PEOPLE'S BEHAVIORS AND VOICES; SHE LOVES TO MAKE BELIEVE.

SHE FINDS OUT A FILM STUDIO IS OPENING IN VIENNA AND THEY ARE LOOKING FOR...

...a "script girl."

SHE HAS NO IDEA WHAT THAT IS, BUT DECIDES TO PLAY HOOKY ONE DAY AND GO FOR IT.

ONCE THERE, SHE (NATURALLY) MANAGES TO LAND A WALK-ON PART IN A MOVIE (EARNING ROUGHLY ENOUGH MONEY TO BUY HERSELF AN ICE-CREAM CONE).

Your gin, Inspector.

SHE GOES BACK HOME AND ANNOUNCES TO HER PARENTS THAT SHE HAS FOUND HER TRUE CALLING AND IS DROPPING OUT OF SCHOOL.

BACK THEN, BERLIN IS THE CAPITAL OF EUROPEAN CINEMA; EVEN THOUGH AN INCREASING NUMBER OF ACTORS CAN FEEL THE WIND CHANGING AND ARE STARTING TO TAKE OFF FOR AMERICA.

Adolf Hitler
Mein Kampf

HEDY LANDS LOTS OF SMALL ROLES AND EVEN ATTRACTS NOTICE FROM THE INTERNATIONAL PRESS.

Mom, Mom! Listen to this! "...Hedy Kiesler, a *charming Austrian girl*"!!

That's great, now go clean your charming room.

New York Times

AND THEN, AT LONG LAST, SHE'S OFFERED THE LEAD PART IN A CZECH FILM TITLED *ECSTASY*. SHE IS SEVENTEEN.

SHE LOVES HOW MODERN THE SCREENPLAY IS.

My character spots a handsome stranger, and it's love at first sight! So she sets out to seduce him, has a fling with him, and then leaves him because, as it turns out, she's married!

H. KIESLER

EKstase

THE FILM IS A HIT RIGHT OUT OF THE GATE, WITH THOUSANDS OF PEOPLE RUSHING TO SEE IT OPENING WEEKEND.

HEDY TRIES TO WARN HER PARENTS: SHE MAKES A FULLY NUDE APPEARANCE IN THE FILM.

WHEN IT COMES TIME FOR THE SCENE WHERE SHE SIMULATES AN ORGASM IN A CLOSE-UP SHOT, HER FATHER STANDS AND LEAVES THE ROOM.

Get your coat, Mother.

THE KIESLER PARENTS ARE FILLED WITH SHAME, BUT THEIR DAUGHTER IS NOW A CELEBRITY.

Fine, just um... just put them wherever.

ONE OF THE WEALTHIEST MEN IN AUSTRIA COURTS HER WITH GREAT ARDOR.

Well, good! I'd much rather see her get married than behaving like a

Emil!!!

FRITZ MANDL IS THE BIGGEST WEAPONS MANUFACTURER IN THE COUNTRY (WITH CLOSE TIES TO THE FASCIST MOVEMENT IN AUSTRIA).

THE NEWLY MARRIED COUPLE ENTERTAINS MANY OF HIS FRIENDS AND CLIENTS.

HEDY, THE TROPHY WIFE, SMILES WHEN SHE HAS TO SMILE. SHE WILL LATER SAY, IN HER AUTOBIOGRAPHY, THAT:

"It's easy to be glamorous. Just stand still and look stupid."

BUT THAT DOESN'T MEAN SHE'S DEAF: SHE DOESN'T MISS A WORD DURING THOSE LONG EVENINGS SPENT DISCUSSING SUBMARINES, TORPEDOES, AND SECRET PLANS.

MEANWHILE, APPEARING ON THE BIG SCREEN EVER AGAIN IS OUT OF THE QUESTION: HER EXTREMELY JEALOUS HUSBAND IS ADAMANTLY AGAINST IT.

HE SPENDS A FORTUNE BUYING UP EVERY EXISTING PRINT OF *ECSTASY* AND DESTROYS THEM.

HE HAS HER FOLLOWED, FORBIDS HER FROM GOING OUT, SPIES ON HER FRIENDS, AND BASICALLY FORCES HER TO LIVE LIKE A CAPTIVE.

HER FATHER DIES OF A HEART ATTACK. HEDY FIGURES THAT LIFE IS SHORT AND THAT SHE NEEDS TO LEAVE FRITZ.

TO GET HER DIVORCE, SHE FIRST TRIES BLACKMAIL.

No, it's nothing... It's just that after all this time, I sort of know a lot about your schemes with the Nazis...

I'm just saying...

EVENTUALLY, SHE SLIPS A FEW SLEEPING PILLS INTO THE MAID'S COFFEE, STEALS HER CLOTHES, AND SNEAKS OFF TO PARIS.

(With a suitcase filled with jewelry.)

SHE BOOKS PASSAGE ON THE *NORMANDIE* AND SETS SAIL FOR AMERICA.

LOUIS B. MAYER, THE CEO OF MGM, JUST HAPPENS (MIRACLE!) TO BE ON BOARD THE SAME SHIP.

Yes. I saw your film, *Ecstasy*.

A woman should really keep her T&A for her husband.

PLAN B: SHE MANAGES TO BECOME PALS WITH MRS. MAYER. PLUS, MR. MAYER IS ABLE TO OBSERVE THE EFFECT HEDY HAS ON JUST ABOUT EVERY MALE ON BOARD.

Oops!

SHE LEAVES THE *NORMANDIE* WITH A SEVEN-YEAR CONTRACT WITH MGM UNDER HER ARM.

MAYER STARTS OFF BY TRYING TO FIND HER A LESS GERMAN-SOUNDING NAME.

There's this young actress who just died, and she had a swell name. Barbara La Marr. What do you think?

A... a *dead* actress??

um...

HEDY *LAMARR* THEN SPENDS SIX MONTHS LEARNING ENGLISH BY WATCHING FILMS. SHE HAS A HARD TIME OF IT.

"Frankly, my dear, I don't give a down." Damn?

BUT HER BREATHTAKING BEAUTY IS UNANIMOUSLY RECOGNIZED AND LANDS HER ROLES ANYWAY.

EVERY TIME SHE APPEARS IN A FILM, SHE STARTS A NEW FASHION TREND IN THE U.S.

Make me a *brunette!*

MEANWHILE, BACK IN HER NATIVE EUROPE, THE NAZIS ARE MAKING HEADWAY. SHE'S HORRIFIED.

"A U-Boat torpedoed a ship full of British refugees, with dozens of children on board."

Oh my God...

SHE FEELS HELPLESS, SO FAR AWAY FROM HER COUNTRY. PLUS, SHE'S *BORED*. SHE DOESN'T DRINK, SHE AVOIDS PARTIES, AND PREFERS TO HOST QUIET DINNERS WITH INTELLIGENT PEOPLE (A RARITY IN HER MILIEU).

Man Ray

AND SO, JUST AS SHE DID WHEN SHE WAS LITTLE, SHE ENTERTAINS HERSELF. SHE MAKES A FULLY EQUIPPED WORKSHOP FOR HERSELF, WHERE SHE COMES UP WITH GADGETS FOR HER HOME.

An automated mustard dispenser! A must!

THOUGH SHE LOVES INVENTING THINGS, MOST OF HER INVENTIONS DON'T ACTUALLY WORK. OVERALL THOUGH, HER IDEAS AREN'T BAD.

SHE TRIES TO MEET AS MANY INTERESTING PEOPLE AS POSSIBLE, WHICH IS HOW SHE ENDS UP SITTING NEXT TO AVANT-GARDE COMPOSER GEORGE ANTHEIL AT A DINNER PARTY ONE NIGHT. HE COMPOSED *BALLET MÉCANIQUE*, WRITTEN FOR SIXTEEN PLAYER PIANOS PLAYING SIMULTANEOUSLY.

THEY TALK ABOUT EVERYTHING UNDER THE SUN, BUT ESPECIALLY ABOUT THE WAR.

I can't stand being here in Hollywood twiddling my thumbs like this! I want to help! I have *tons* of great ideas for the U.S. Army!

har har... er... *you*??

HEDY EXPLAINS THAT, FROM WHAT SHE CAN UNDERSTAND, THE U.S. TORPEDOES ALWAYS MISS THEIR TARGETS WHEN AIMING AT A NAZI SUB.

They need to be remote-controlled! By radio!

Yes, but then the signal would be intercepted!

THEY OFTEN PLAY MUSIC TOGETHER: ONE WOULD IMPROVISE A TUNE THAT THE OTHER HAD TO FOLLOW BEFORE CHANGING IT AND THEN BEING ACCOMPANIED IN TURN (AND SO ON AND SO FORTH).

IT'S DURING ONE OF THOSE LITTLE GAMES OF MUSICAL PING-PONG THAT A FLOW OF DISCONNECTED IDEAS SUDDENLY CONNECT.

... Hedy? ...

What...what if the transmitter and the receiver...communicated by constantly changing from one frequency to another...both at the same time... Then their signal couldn't be jammed, right?

George! You managed to have sixteen player pianos play at the same time. Why not two radios??

STRANGELY ENOUGH, IT MAKES SENSE. SO GEORGE HELPS HEDY FLESH OUT HER IDEA AND, MORE IMPORTANTLY, APPLY IT. THEY WORK ON THE PROJECT ALL THROUGH THE FALL OF 1940.

MEANWHILE, HEDY HAS THREE MORE IDEAS FOR MILITARY TECHNOLOGY, NAMELY MUNITIONS THAT WILL EXPLODE NEAR BIG METAL OBJECTS.

AT CHRISTMAS, SHE FILES FOR A PATENT FOR THE FREQUENCY-HOPPING TECHNOLOGY (BUT NOT UNDER HER STAGE NAME, SO AS NOT TO INFLUENCE THE COMMITTEE). GEORGE PROOFREADS HER CORRESPONDENCE, FOR HEDY WRITES ALMOST PHONETICALLY.

Hey! I dropped out of school at sixteen, you know!

And I speak four languages!

(NATURALLY, NONE OF THIS KEEPS HER FROM DOING ONE FILM AFTER ANOTHER.)

ZIEGFELD GIRL, WITH JUDY GARLAND AND LANA TURNER

HEDY OFFERS HER "SECRET COMMUNICATION SYSTEM" TO THE ARMY. THEY ARE INTRIGUED BUT DON'T REALLY GET THE CONCEPT.

That's nice, doll, but...how are you going to fit a *piano* into a radio?

THEY SUGGEST SHE HELP AMERICA IN A WAY MORE IN TUNE WITH HER NATURAL ABILITIES.

A pretty young thing like you!

SO HEDY TAKES PART IN EFFORTS TO PROVIDE MORAL SUPPORT TO THE TROOPS AND IN THE SALE OF WAR BONDS.

SURE ENOUGH, SHE RAISES TWENTY-FIVE MILLION DOLLARS.

But my frequency-hopping system would have been a thousand times more useful to you!!

THE NAVY FILES HER BLUEPRINTS AWAY IN A DRAWER (AFTER LABELING IT TOP SECRET FOR SEVENTEEN YEARS, JUST IN CASE). ONCE AGAIN, HEDY IS FRUSTRATED AS HELL AT NOT BEING TAKEN SERIOUSLY.

ESPECIALLY SINCE HER HOLLYWOOD CAREER IS INCREASINGLY UNFULFILLING: SHE TRIES HER HAND AT COMEDIES AND THRILLERS, AND EVEN PRODUCES TWO FILMS...

(Cecil B. DeMille's *Samson and Delilah*)

...BUT SHE'S ALWAYS TYPECAST IN THE ROLE OF THE MYSTERIOUS, DIAPHANOUS FEMME FATALE.

SHE TURNS DOWN ROLES (E.G. INGRID BERGMAN'S ROLE IN *CASABLANCA*), ABHORS INTERVIEWS, AND EVEN RECEIVES THE 1949 SOUR APPLE AWARD FOR LEAST COOPERATIVE ACTRESS.

THIS WHOLE TIME, SHE PLOWS THROUGH A SUCCESSION OF LOVERS (CHAPLIN, BRANDO, CAPA), MARRIES FIVE MORE TIMES, AND HAS THREE CHILDREN.

James

Anthony

Denise

SHE ALWAYS GOES FOR THE SAME TYPE OF MAN: INTELLIGENT, BROODING, AND OLDER THAN HER.

"Men under thirty-five have too much to learn. And I don't have time to teach them."

HER AUTOBIOGRAPHY, WHICH TALKS ABOUT HER LOVE AFFAIRS, WILL BE CONSIDERED ONE OF THE TEN MOST EROTIC MEMOIRS OF ALL TIME BY *PLAYBOY* MAGAZINE.

ITS PREFACE IS EVEN PENNED BY A PSYCHIATRIST WARNING READERS ABOUT THE DEPRAVED DIVORCEE'S PATHOLOGICAL LIBIDO.

YEARS PASS. HER PATENT IS EVENTUALLY DECLASSIFIED. A MILITARY ENGINEER COMES ACROSS IT AND CAN'T UNDERSTAND WHY NOBODY EVER USED SUCH A REVOLUTIONARY INVENTION.

THE ARMY (FINALLY!) HAS THE IDEA TO APPLY IT TO ITS RADAR. AND THE TECHNOLOGY IS SOON BORROWED EVERYWHERE FOR COMMERCIAL USES...

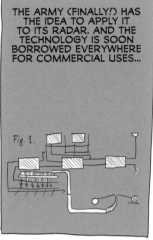

Fig.1.

...TO THE POINT WHERE IT IS USED TO DEVELOP GPS AND WIFI (AMONG OTHER TECHNOLOGIES).

HEDY FOLLOWS ALL THIS CLOSELY AND WITH GREAT PRIDE, EVEN THOUGH HER NAME ISN'T MENTIONED (AND NATURALLY SHE NEVER SEES A DIME).

New Scientist

BETRAYED BY HER FADING LOOKS, AND NEVER HAVING BEEN TRULY RECOGNIZED FOR ANYTHING ELSE, HEDY LIVES AS A RECLUSE IN FLORIDA AND EXPERIMENTS WITH COSMETIC SURGERY TO VARYING DEGREES OF SUCCESS.

UNTIL THE DAY WHEN, IN 1996, THE ELECTRONIC FRONTIER FOUNDATION DECIDES TO HONOR HER FOR HER SCIENTIFIC CONTRIBUTION.

Well.

It's about time!

HEDY IS THRILLED AND FLATTERED. BUT SHE OPTS TO SEND HER SON TO ACCEPT THE TROPHY FOR HER, SO AS TO AVOID SHOWING HER AGING FACE. AT EIGHTY-TWO, SHE'S STILL COMING UP WITH INVENTIONS SUCH AS NEW TRAFFIC LIGHTS OR PHOSPHORESCENT DOG COLLARS, AND SHE WRITES TO THE AVIATION INDUSTRY WITH SUGGESTIONS ON HOW TO IMPROVE THE CONCORDE.

SHE GIVES HERSELF ONE LAST OBJECTIVE: TO LIVE UNTIL THE NEW MILLENNIUM. SHE DIES IN HER SLEEP ON JANUARY 19, 2000.

Her ashes are scattered over the Viennese forest.

HER OBITUARY PRAISES HER UNBELIEVABLE BEAUTY, BARELY MENTIONING HER BRILLIANT AND INVENTIVE MIND.

BUT TODAY, IN HER NATIVE AUSTRIA AND SEVERAL OTHER COUNTRIES, INVENTORS' DAY IS CELEBRATED EVERY YEAR ON HER BIRTHDAY.

Pénélope *

NAZIQ AL-ABID

ACTIVIST ARISTOCRAT

1898 - 1959

NAZIQ IS BORN IN 1898, INTO A WEALTHY MERCHANT FAMILY FROM DAMASCUS, SYRIA.

THE AL-ABIDS ARE VERY WELL REGARDED IN THE OTTOMAN EMPIRE (OF WHICH SYRIA HAS BEEN PART FOR CENTURIES). HER FATHER HAS JUST BEEN APPOINTED GOVERNOR OF MASUL, AND HER UNCLE IS AN ADVISOR TO THE SULTAN.

Abdulhamid II

HER PARENTS ARE RICH, AND NAZIQ HAS IT EASY:

صباح الخير

Hello

Bonjour

Guten Tag

BUT SHE ISN'T LIKE HER SISTERS.

SHE UNDERSTANDS EARLY ON HOW PRIVILEGED SHE IS AND DOESN'T FEEL COMFORTABLE WITH SUCH AN UNFAIR ADVANTAGE.

Naziq! Dinner's ready!

I'm eating with the servants!! You can't stop me!

(SHE ALSO INSISTS ON WORKING IN THE FIELDS.)

MOST OF ALL, THOUGH, SHE FEELS INCREASING HATRED TOWARD THE OTTOMAN EMPIRE.

You mustn't say such things, honey. The sultan is very good to our family!

But I'm proud of you for defending your Kurdish roots.

Don't ever forget them.

HER FATHER WANTS HER TO GET AN EDUCATION, AND SENDS HER TO ISTANBUL.

To study agriculture!

255

BUT AS SOON AS SHE ARRIVES, SHE REBELS: SHE ORGANIZES A PROTEST DENOUNCING THE DISCRIMINATION BY TURKISH TEACHERS AGAINST ARAB STUDENTS.

BUT SHE'S THE ONE WHO IS LET GO. (AND SHIPPED BACK TO SYRIA.)

SHE STARTS WRITING OP-ED PIECES (USING A MALE PSEUDONYM) IN THE LOCAL PRESS THAT CRITICIZE THE OTTOMAN EMPIRE FOR KEEPING ALL THE GOOD JOBS FOR THEMSELVES INSTEAD OF SPREADING THEM EQUALLY AMONG ARABS AND TURKS.

THE COLONIALISTS MUST GO!

CONVINCED SHE ISN'T ALONE, AT THE AGE OF SIXTEEN SHE RECRUITS OTHER GIRLS AS FED UP AS SHE IS...

Who's with me?!!!

...AND FOUNDS AN ADVOCATE GROUP FOR WOMEN'S RIGHTS IN SYRIA.

BUT THIS DOESN'T GO OVER WELL WITH THE OTTOMAN GOVERNOR OF DAMASCUS, WHO EXILES HER (ALONG WITH HER FAMILY) TO EGYPT.

Way to go, Naziq!

BUT WITH WWI COMES THE FALL OF THE OTTOMAN EMPIRE.

Ha!!

NAZIQ GOES HOME.

DURING THE POST-OTTOMAN RECONSTRUCTION PERIOD, WHERE EVERYTHING SEEMS POSSIBLE, NAZIQ'S FERVOR REACHES NEW HEIGHTS, AND SHE DISCOVERS A NEW CAUSE:

...THE WOMEN'S RIGHT TO VOTE.

Worth a shot!

You never know!

SHE THEN FOUNDS THE FIRST WOMEN'S NGO IN SYRIA: NOOR AL-FAYHA ("THE LIGHT OF DAMASCUS"),

(age 21)

AS WELL AS A FEMINIST MAGAZINE OF THE SAME NAME.

THAT YEAR, U.S. PRESIDENT WILSON SENDS AN AMERICAN DELEGATION* TO SYRIA TO SURVEY ITS NATIONALS ABOUT THEIR FEELINGS ON THE FUTURE OF THEIR COUNTRY. AFTER FOUR HUNDRED YEARS OF OTTOMAN OCCUPATION, MANY NATIONS HAVE THEIR SIGHTS SET ON THE NEWLY FREED SYRIA, FRANCE IN PARTICULAR...

(*the King-Crane Commission)

THIS IS A GOLDEN OPPORTUNITY FOR NAZIQ AND HER FELLOW INTELLECTUALS TO PRESENT THEIR PROJECT TO THE AMERICANS.

It's just that..

no veil ↓

...even in the U.S. women can't vote...

Well then, it's high time, wouldn't you say?

DURING THIS SAME TIME, SHE ALSO FOUNDS THE SYRIAN RED CRESCENT, AFTER THE RED CROSS MODEL, TO PROVIDE ASSISTANCE TO THE WAR WOUNDED.

BENDING TO MILITARY PRESSURE, KING FAISAL I CEDES IN JULY OF 1920, AGREEING TO PLACE SYRIA UNDER FRENCH MANDATE.

AT THIS TIME, NAZIQ ANSWERS THE CALL MADE BY DEFENSE MINISTER YUSEF AL-AZMEH, WHO REFUSES TO SURRENDER PEACEFULLY.

THE LITTLE UPPER-CLASS LADY TAKES TO ARMS.

SHE PARADES DOWN THE STREETS OF DAMASCUS IN UNIFORM. (SCANDALOUS!)

SHE POSES FOR FOREIGN JOURNALISTS, WHO NICKNAME HER THE "JOAN OF ARC OF THE ARABS."

DURING THE FIERCE BATTLE OF MAYSALUN, THE OUTNUMBERED REBELS ARE MASSACRED BY THE FRENCH ARMY.

NAZIQ IS ONE OF THE ONLY SURVIVORS.

HER BRAVERY DURING COMBAT EARNS HER THE NEW RANK OF GENERAL IN THE SYRIAN ARMY. (SHE IS THE FIRST WOMAN TO EVER BEAR THAT TITLE, OBVIOUSLY.)

BE THAT AS IT MAY, FRANCE IS NOW RUNNING HER COUNTRY.

SHE'S PROMPTLY EXILED TO ISTANBUL.

I'm having déja vu.

IN 1922, FRANCE GRANTS HER PERMISSION TO RETURN TO SYRIA, PROVIDED SHE GIVES UP POLITICS.

SHE PROMISES TO STICK TO HUMANITARIAN ACTIVITIES.

SHE AND TWO OTHER FEMINIST ACTIVISTS (FROM LEBANON) FOUND THE WOMEN'S UNION.

THE FRENCH KICK HER OUT AGAIN (TO JORDAN, THIS TIME).

IN 1925, SHE SNEAKS BACK IN TO JOIN THE RESISTANCE AGAINST FRANCE.

SABOTAGE, STEALING MUNITIONS, RESCUE MISSIONS—SHE LIVES LIKE AN OUTLAW.

SHE FOUNDS THE DAMASCENE WOMEN'S AWAKENING SOCIETY, TO EDUCATE WIDOWS FROM RURAL SYRIA.

(THEY OFFER WORKSHOPS, ENGLISH LESSONS, AND ENCOURAGE WOMEN TO COMPLETE THEIR EDUCATION.)

IN 1927, THE FRENCH EXPEL HER ONCE AGAIN.

Don't bother, I know the way out.

IN LEBANON, SHE RECONNECTS WITH MUHAMMAD JAMIL BAYHUM, A SYRIAN POLITICIAN WHO SUPPORTED HER WOMEN'S SUFFRAGE PROJECT.

Naziq, *of course* I'm a feminist!

NAZIQ EVENTUALLY AGREES TO MARRY HIM (AT THE RIPE OLD AGE OF THIRTY, WHICH IS UNHEARD OF IN CONSERVATIVE SYRIA).

I was fine on my own before!

IMPRESSED BY HIS WIFE'S DEDICATION, MUHAMMAD FUNDS ALL HER POLITICAL PROJECTS, INCLUDING THE PUBLICATION OF FEMINIST AUTHORS.

IN LEBANON IN 1935, SHE CREATES THE ASSOCIATION OF WORKING WOMEN.

Equal pay! Maternity leave!

THEN, FOLLOWING THE ARAB-ISRAELI WAR OF 1948, SHE CREATES AN ORGANIZATION AIMED AT FINDING WORK FOR PALESTINIAN REFUGEES.

Oh, and I'll also be funding the construction of a children's hospital!

Just keeping busy.

MEANWHILE, SHE ADOPTS THREE ORPHANS. SHE MAKES THEM STUDY HARD AND TEACHES THEM TO DEFEND THE WEAK.

He was bullying a little boy, Mom!

NAZIQ PASSES AWAY AT THE AGE OF SIXTY-ONE. AT HER FUNERAL, WRITERS AND INTELLECTUALS LINE UP TO PRAISE HER HEROISM, SO INTRICATELY LINKED TO THE HISTORY OF HER COUNTRY.

PREDESTINED FOR A QUIET LIFE OF LUXURY, SHE LEFT HER UPPER-CLASS COCOON TO HELP HER PEOPLE'S VOICE BE HEARD.

THE MEN AND WOMEN WHO CROSSED PATHS WITH HER ALL AGREED THAT IT WAS THROUGH HER FRIENDLINESS AND COMPASSION THAT SHE ALWAYS MANAGED TO UNITE AND PERSUADE.

Her name, in fact, means "gentle and courteous."

BUT IT WAS BECAUSE OF HER DETERMINATION THAT SHE TRIUMPHED EVERY TIME THEY TRIED TO SILENCE HER.

IN HER TIRELESS FIGHT FOR JUSTICE, WHENEVER THEY SHOWED HER THE DOOR, SHE CAME BACK IN THROUGH THE WINDOW.

SYRIA

NAZIQ AL-ABID .20

(A big thank-you to Rim Lariani for her help with the translation!)

259

Pénélope

FRANCES GLESSNER LEE
CRIME MINIATURIST

1878-1962

FRANCES GLESSNER IS BORN IN CHICAGO ON MARCH 25, 1878. EVERYBODY CALLS HER FANNY.

SHE DOESN'T GO TO SCHOOL AND INSTEAD PASSES THE TIME DOING WHAT PROPER YOUNG LADIES DO: SHE SEWS, SHE EMBROIDERS, AND, FOLLOWING ONE OF THE PUREST OF VICTORIAN TRADITIONS, SHE MAKES MINIATURES.

HER BROTHER GOES OFF TO HARVARD TO STUDY MEDICINE. SHE WOULD LOVE TO FOLLOW SUIT, BUT NATURALLY THAT IS OUT OF THE QUESTION.

Come now, darling. A young woman at university? Ha ha.

AT NINETEEN, SHE MARRIES AN ATTORNEY NAMED BLEWETT LEE. THEY HAVE THREE CHILDREN.

SHE'S FRUSTRATED AND UNHAPPY, FOR SHE WANTS TO BE USEFUL TO SOCIETY.

SO SHE KEEPS BUSY. FOR HER MOTHER'S BIRTHDAY, SHE MAKES A MINIATURE OF THE CHICAGO SYMPHONY ORCHESTRA.

(ninety musicians, their instruments, and their sheet music)
↓

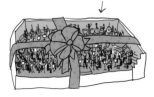

SHE ALSO LATCHES ON TO HER BROTHER AND HIS DOCTOR FRIENDS AND LISTENS TO THEIR STORIES.

George, his best friend →

GEORGE IS INTERESTED IN FORENSIC MEDICINE AND TELLS FANNY HOW HARD IT IS TO DO HIS JOB RIGHT.

Policemen at the crime scenes aren't required to have the slightest bit of training on the issue. They move the body and tramp through the blood, completely careless.

It's hopeless.

HE EXPLAINS TO HER THAT THERE'S ACTUALLY A METHOD, A SPECIFIC WAY TO EXAMINE THE BODY AND THE SCENE.

Unforgivable mistakes are being made! So many murderers are running around free because of them! *Tsk-tsk...*

IN THOSE DAYS, NOBODY CALLS THESE THINGS INTO QUESTION.

Hey, I find a body, I pick it up, I clean up, end of story!

I'm a busy man.

IN PARTICULAR, MANY WOMEN FOUND DEAD IN THEIR HOMES ARE WRITTEN OFF AS "SUICIDE" CASES, BY DEFAULT.

I'm *devastated*.

FANNY IS FASCINATED BY THE SUBJECT AND ASKS MORE AND MORE QUESTIONS (AND DOESN'T SHY AWAY FROM ALL THE GORY DETAILS).

But...how could the crowbar be jammed into the—

Okay, Fanny, time for you to go now.

AFTER SIXTEEN YEARS OF MARRIAGE, SHE GETS A DIVORCE.

HER BROTHER DIES. THEN HER MOTHER. THEN HER FATHER. SHE INHERITS ALL HER FAMILY'S MONEY.

GLESSNER

MILLIONS OF DOLLARS, IT TURNS OUT, AMASSED BY HER FATHER VIA HIS MANUFACTURING BUSINESS.

Wow, well okay then.

SHE IS FIFTY-FIVE YEARS OLD.

AFTER YEARS OF FEELING USELESS, FANNY KNOWS *EXACTLY* WHAT SHE'S GOING TO DO WITH ALL THAT MONEY (AND ALL HER FREE TIME).

Reform forensic science in this country!!

Just like that.

SHE STARTS OUT BY MAKING A COLOSSAL DONATION TO HARVARD SO THAT THEY CAN (FINALLY!) CREATE A CURRICULUM IN THIS FIELD, AS WELL AS AN IMPRESSIVE LIBRARY ON THE TOPIC.

Interpreting Blood Splatter

Book 1

NATURALLY, SHE ARRANGES FOR HER OLD FRIEND GEORGE TO CHAIR THE NEW DEPARTMENT (AND SHE DOESN'T MISS A CLASS).

HE DIES TWO YEARS LATER. FANNY IS NOW PRACTICALLY AN EXPERT ON THE TOPIC.

After all this time, I do know my way around the subject.

SHE FOUNDS THE HARVARD ASSOCIATES IN POLICE SCIENCE (HAPS) AND ORGANIZES WEEKLONG SEMINARS TO TEACH POLICEMEN AND DOCTORS HOW TO "INTERROGATE" A CRIME SCENE.

SHE ADVOCATES A "GEOMETRIC" SEARCH.

You have to look all around you, clockwise. And not disregard anything, not even the trash.

(Write that down!)

HOWEVER, IT'S DIFFICULT TO PUT ALL THIS INTO PRACTICE, SINCE THERE'S NO WAY OF TAKING HER DISCIPLES TO "REAL" CRIME SCENES.

Okay, let's say the pencil is me. The ink is the gas stove.

IN ORDER FOR THEM TO TEST THEIR SHERLOCK HOLMES SKILLS, FANNY HAS THE IDEA TO MAKE MINIATURE REPLICAS OF REAL CRIME SCENES.

THEY'RE WHAT SHE CALLS "NUTSHELL STUDIES OF UNEXPLAINED DEATHS."

FOR THE ACTUAL FACTS, FANNY CAREFULLY FOLLOWS THE POLICE AND AUTOPSY REPORTS.

SHE DUPLICATES THE ANGLE OF THE WEAPON'S ENTRY, THE POSITION OF THE BODY, THE BLOOD SPLATTER...

AS FOR THE REST, ALL THE NON-CRUCIAL DETAILS, SHE HAS A BALL.

267

SHE SPENDS THREE MONTHS ON HER FIRST NUTSHELL STUDY (1943), ENTITLED "THE HANGED FARMER."

THREE MONTHS, BECAUSE FANNY DOESN'T LEAVE OUT A SINGLE DETAIL.

exact time of death

potato peels in the sink

labels on the jars

dishtowels in the drawers

real newspaper headlines from that day

FANNY IS UNCOMPROMISING. EVERYTHING HAS TO MATCH REALITY: HER LOCKS REALLY DO LOCK WITH TINY KEYS, THE LAMPS ACTUALLY TURN ON, AND THE CLOTHES SHE MAKES ARE IDENTICAL.

knitting with straight pins

AS FOR CLUES TO UNCOVER, THEY'RE HIDDEN EVERYWHERE.

a bullet lodged in the wall

an ashtray turned upside down

a lipstick mark under the pillow

EVEN IN THE HUE OF THE SKIN, DEPENDING ON THE STATE OF DECOMPOSITION.

PARTICIPANTS HAVE NINETY MINUTES TO STUDY THE SCENE.

THE GOAL ISN'T NECESSARILY TO SOLVE THE CASE LIKE IN A GAME OF CLUE, BUT TO PRACTICE INTELLIGENT OBSERVATION.

AT FIRST, POLICEMEN ARE *VERY* RELUCTANT TO ACCEPT THIS SELF-TAUGHT GRANNY...

...BUT THE EFFICIENCY OF HER APPROACH ENDS UP WINNING THEM OVER.

SHE IS MADE AN HONORARY CAPTAIN IN THE NEW HAMPSHIRE STATE POLICE.

(SHE IS THE FIRST WOMAN TO EARN THAT TITLE.)

SHE DIES AT THE AGE OF EIGHTY-FOUR. HARVARD CLOSES DOWN THE DEPARTMENT OF LEGAL MEDICINE AND THROWS OUT THE NUTSHELL STUDIES.

(There are about twenty of them.)

BUT A PROFESSOR SALVAGES AND RESTORES THEM, AND THEN USES THEM TO TRAIN THE MARYLAND POLICE FORCE.

GRADUALLY, THE ENTIRE COUNTRY WILL EMBRACE THIS FIELD OF EXPERTISE, AND, MORE IMPORTANTLY, CHANGE EXISTING CRIME SCENE PROCEDURES (AND TRAIN FORENSICS EXPERTS).

CRIME SCENE DO NOT CROSS

TODAY, HAPS CONTINUES TO ORGANIZE SEMINARS TWICE A YEAR. THE NUTSHELL STUDIES HAVE NOT BEEN STORED AWAY IN A MUSEUM— THEY'RE STILL BEING USED BY CRIMINOLOGISTS AS A TEACHING TOOL.

The sets are dated, but the level of precision remains unparalleled, even by virtual simulation.

TODAY, EXPERTS RELY ON DNA ANALYSIS AND HIGHLY ADVANCED TECHNOLOGY. IT'S HARD TO BELIEVE THAT LESS THAN ONE HUNDRED YEARS AGO, DOCTORS HAD TO FIGHT FOR ATTENTION TO BE PAID TO EVIDENCE.

Oops!

FOR FANNY, THIS WAS ALL JUST A HOBBY, NOTHING MORE. SHE NEVER GOT HER COLLEGE DEGREE. BUT SHE LOVED THE FINE DETAILS AND STORIES FILLED WITH MISSING PIECES TO CONNECT.

SHE WAS THE MAIN INSPIRATION FOR THE CHARACTER OF JESSICA FLETCHER IN THE POPULAR *MURDER, SHE WROTE* TV SERIES.

Pénelope *

MAE JEMISON
ASTRONAUT

1956–

MAE CAROL JEMISON IS BORN ON OCTOBER 17, 1956 IN ALABAMA.

PEOPLE NICKNAME HER ROSEBUD BECAUSE OF HER PRETTY LIPS.

SHE'S AFRAID OF THE DARK, OF HEIGHTS, OF THE BASEMENT— OF EVERYTHING.

BUT AS THE YOUNGEST SIBLING, SHE HAS TO LEARN HOW TO BE CUNNING AND NIMBLE TO SURVIVE.

IN KINDERGARTEN SHE STATES SHE WANTS TO BECOME "SCIENTIFIC."

You mean a nurse?

No, scientific! Like the mad scientists!

HER FAMILY MOVES TO ONE OF CHICAGO'S ROUGH NEIGHBORHOODS, WHERE GANG WARS ARE RAGING.

At home, when we hear gunshots, we turn off the lights and get down on the floor.

HER MOTHER PROTECTS HER KIDS LIKE A MAMA BEAR TO KEEP THEM ON THE STRAIGHT AND NARROW.

You come near my boy again and I'll make myself a purse out of the skin on your ass.

Yes, Ma'am.

EVENTUALLY, THEY MOVE TO A NEIGHBORHOOD WHERE SHE'S THE ONLY BLACK GIRL.

MAE IS ALWAYS ASKING HER MOM (WHO HAS BETTER THINGS TO DO) A MILLION QUESTIONS. THE ANSWER IS ALWAYS:

Figure it out. Look it up.

AS A TEEN, SHE HAS TWO GREAT PASSIONS IN LIFE:

Mom!! I wanna take dance lessons!!

Space. The final frontier.

And I want a telescope, too!!!

HER PARENTS DON'T HAVE THE MEANS TO BUY HER ONE, SO MAE PRACTICALLY CAMPS OUT AT THE PLANETARIUM.

WHEN SHE LOOKS UP INTO SPACE, HER FEARS OF THE DARK AND OF HEIGHTS VANISH.

DURING THAT SAME PERIOD, SHE BECOMES A HARD-CORE SCI-FI AND COMICS FAN.

I'd say I'm a cross between Catwoman and Spock.

BUT IN THE NOVELS SHE READS, THE INTERESTING CHARACTERS ARE NEVER GIRLS AND NEVER BLACK.

Let alone *black girls*!

ISAAC ASIMOV

AT THE DINNER TABLE, HER FAMILY TALKS ABOUT POLITICS, CIVIL RIGHTS, STOKELY CARMICHAEL, AND MALCOLM X.

Don't say you're "colored" anymore, Mae. You're *black*.

MS. MARVEL

HER MOTHER TEACHES HER THAT THEY ARE BEAUTIFUL JUST AS THEY ARE, AND THAT GOING FORWARD, THEY'LL WEAR THEIR NATURAL HAIR WITH PRIDE.

BUT HER FATHER ALSO TEACHES HER THAT HER DUTY IS TO EXCEL.

As a black girl, you're going to have to be twice as good as a white man to get where you want to go.

MARTIN LUTHER KING JR. IS ASSASSINATED. RIOTS BREAK OUT IN MAE'S NEIGHBORHOOD. POLICEMEN ARE ALLOWED TO SHOOT TO KILL IF NECESSARY. A THIRTEEN-YEAR-OLD BOY IS GUNNED DOWN IN THE STREET.

MAE REALIZES HER LIFE ISN'T WORTH A THING. EVEN THOUGH SHE'S SMART AND FUNNY AND PRETTY, SHE COULD BE PUT DOWN LIKE A DOG.

AND SHE'S SCARED.

BUT AFTER A FEW DAYS OF HIDING OUT, SHE STARTS TO BOIL WITH *RAGE*.

I come from women *and* slaves! My ancestors had *NO* rights! But I'm part of this country! I *matter!!*

IN HIGH SCHOOL, MAE IS A GIFTED ATHLETE. SHE'S ALSO VERY, VERY GOOD AT SCIENCE. HER CURIOSITY IS INSATIABLE.

FOR HER SCIENCE PROJECT, SHE FOCUSES ON A GENETIC DISEASE THAT AFFECTS A LOT OF AFRICAN AMERICANS: SICKLE CELL ANEMIA.

HER MOTHER HELPS HER IN THE USUAL WAY.

Figure it out.

Look it up.

SHE BOLDLY CALLS UP COOK COUNTY HOSPITAL WITH HER QUESTIONS.

It would be easier if you just stopped by our lab. Say tomorrow at three?

THERE, SHE IS RECEIVED BY LAB DIRECTORS WHO TELL HER SHE CAN STAY AND OBSERVE AS LONG AS SHE WANTS BUT WHO REFUSE TO GIVE HER ANY ANSWERS.

What is *your* theory, Mae?

SO SHE DOES HER RESEARCH.

TO UNDERSTAND SOME ARTICLES, SHE HAS TO READ OTHERS, THEN OTHERS, AND SO ON AND SO FORTH. SHE WORKS NONSTOP.

SHE'S ONLY FIFTEEN, BUT THE RESEARCHERS TREAT HER LIKE AN ADULT.

SHE WINS FIRST PRIZE IN CHICAGO'S SCIENCE CONTEST.

HER MATH TEACHER AGREES TO GIVE HER EXTRA LESSONS AFTER CLASS.

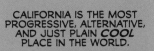

Seriously?

Laugh all you want

AFTER GRADUATION, SEVERAL PRESTIGIOUS UNIVERSITIES TRY TO GET HER TO ENROLL (WITH OFFERS OF SCHOLARSHIPS).

Stanford! It's a no-brainer!!

Why so far away, honey, boo hoo

TAKING OFF FOR CALIFORNIA ALL BY HERSELF AT SIXTEEN IS TERRIFYING.

BUT SHE KNOWS SHE'S HEADING FOR HER DREAM SCHOOL IN HER DREAM STATE.

CALIFORNIA IS THE MOST PROGRESSIVE, ALTERNATIVE, AND JUST PLAIN *COOL* PLACE IN THE WORLD.

FOUR YEARS LATER, SHE GRADUATES WITH A DOUBLE MAJOR IN CHEMICAL ENGINEERING AND AFRICAN AMERICAN STUDIES.

SHE SPECIALIZES IN AFRICAN DANCE, SWAHILI, SUB-SAHARAN POLITICS...

...and Russian!

It could come in handy for space travel.

BUT SHE STARTS TO REALIZE THAT THERE ARE MANY OBSTACLES DUE TO THE TRIFECTA OF BEING:

A GIRL +

BLACK +

FROM A MODEST BACKGROUND.

PEOPLE ALWAYS ASSUME SHE MUST NOT BE THAT BRIGHT.

Look around! Do you see any others? No? Well there you go!

AND SO, TO CONVINCE HERSELF SHE BELONGS THERE, SHE HOLDS ONTO THE ONE THING SHE NEVER DOUBTED:

I *know* I'm smart.

AFTER STANFORD, SHE GOES TO MED SCHOOL IN NEW YORK (A VERY MALE-DOMINATED PROGRAM).

SHE'S LOOKED DOWN UPON ON THE EAST COAST EVEN *MORE* THAN IN CALIFORNIA.

BUT HER FIRST NIGHT THERE, AT A STUDENT POKER GAME, SHE CLEANS OUT HER CLASSMATES.

So, are the girls losing?

No, the women are winning.

AND THAT SHUTS THEM UP.

SHE'S WORKING ABOUT FORTY TIMES HARDER THAN AT STANFORD.

I'm finding out you can remain efficient after thirty-six hours with no sleep.

THEN, SHE MAKES A CHILDHOOD DREAM COME TRUE WHEN SHE DOES HER INTERNSHIP IN KENYA.

Africa!! For *real*!!! It's not a concept! These are my roots!!

SHE TRAINS AT FREE CLINICS, SPEAKS (FINALLY!) SWAHILI, HAS HER HAIR DONE, EATS TONS OF GREAT FOOD, TRAVELS ALONE TO NEIGHBORING COUNTRIES...

Go back to *New York*???

...AND HAS HERSELF A LITTLE EXISTENTIAL CRISIS.

SHE OFFERS HER SERVICES TO ALL THE NGOS WORKING IN AFRICA.

Doctor, engineer, heck, even babysitter... who cares? Whatever you need!

SHE ENDS UP WITH THE PEACE CORPS, IN LIBERIA AND SIERRA LEONE.

SHE TREATS THE WORST HEMORRHAGING VIRUSES, WITHOUT EQUIPMENT OR MEDICINE.

MAE FEELS A LITTLE LOST. SHE KNOWS THAT DEEP DOWN, SHE DOESN'T WANT TO PRACTICE MEDICINE.

What I really love is science and unknown worlds. Sort of like Mr. Spock. Know what I mean?

SHE HASN'T THOUGHT ABOUT HER CHILDHOOD DREAM IN AGES.

I mean, why not? Because no other black girls have done it before me?

AT THE TIME, NASA IS RECRUITING. AFTER DECADES OF SENDING OUT THE MESSAGE "WHITE MEN ONLY," THEY ARE LOOKING TO ADD MORE DIVERSITY TO THEIR RANKS.

NASA

MAE APPLIES WITHOUT MUCH HOPE.

ONE YEAR LATER, SHE GETS A RESPONSE:

"Everything about your background— chemistry, humanitarian work, dance— *everything* is of interest to us."

SO WITH HER CAT UNDER HER ARM, SHE MOVES TO HOUSTON, TEXAS.

HER TRAINING IS EXTREMELY PHYSICAL AND FEATURES, AMONG OTHER THINGS, SURVIVAL TRAINING IN HOSTILE ENVIRONMENTS.

BUT SHE HAS FINALLY MADE IT.

THE FIRST THING MAE SEES THROUGH THE WINDOW OF THE *STS-47* SPACELAB...

That's Chicago! ♥

SHE THINKS TO HERSELF THAT, STRANGELY ENOUGH, SHE ALWAYS KNEW SHE WOULD END UP THERE AT SOME POINT.

SHE IS THE FIRST BLACK WOMAN IN SPACE.

AFTER SIX YEARS OF MISSIONS, MAE LEAVES NASA. BACK ON EARTH, SHE TEACHES CLASSES IN ENVIRONMENTAL STUDIES.

We must connect technology with social problems. And get everyone involved!

DR. JEMISON

SHE FOUNDS A SCIENCE CAMP FOR KIDS AGES TWELVE TO SIXTEEN.

THE EARTH WE SHARE SUMMER CAMP

AND ONE DAY, SHE SHOWS UP AT A *STAR TREK* CONVENTION.

No, I mean it's funny because I really *am* an astronaut!*

(*in Klingon)

AND THANKS TO THAT ENCOUNTER, MAE JEMISON BECOMES THE FIRST PERSON TO TRAVEL INTO SPACE *AND* GUEST STAR IN AN EPISODE OF *STAR TREK*.

Pénélope ☀

THE SPECTACULAR DR. JEMISON

PEGGY GUGGENHEIM
LOVER OF MODERN ART

1898–1979

MARGUERITE "PEGGY" GUGGENHEIM IS BORN IN AN UPSCALE MANHATTAN NEIGHBORHOOD. SHE'S A PRODUCT OF THE TWO WEALTHIEST JEWISH FAMILIES IN AMERICA (WHO HAVE A MUTUAL DISDAIN FOR EACH OTHER).

Nouveau riche!

SHE'S PRECOCIOUS AND FIGURES OUT HOW ADULT LIFE WORKS EARLY ON.

You're late, Papa. Are you having an affair?

INDEED HE IS, AND IT IS TO ONE OF HIS MISTRESSES, IN FACT, THAT HE OFFERS HIS LIFEJACKET ON THE *TITANIC*.

I die, but I die a gentleman.

SHE'S INCONSOLABLE AND WILL SPEND THE REST OF HER LIFE LOOKING FOR A SUBSTITUTE FATHER FIGURE.

NOW THAT HER FATHER IS GONE, HER UNCLES TURN THEIR BACKS ON HER BRANCH OF THE FAMILY TREE.

THE INSECURITY OF NOT BEING A "REAL" GUGGENHEIM WILL ALSO PLAGUE HER FOREVER.

ON TOP OF THAT, PEGGY FEELS UGLY.

too skinny

too fat

shaved off her eyebrows just "to try it"

anorexic

hates her face

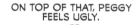

SHE HAS HER NOSE DONE. IT'S A DISASTER AND SHE HIDES FROM THE WORLD FOR WEEKS.

IT'S PARTLY BECAUSE OF HER PRIVILEGED BACKGROUND THAT SHE INSISTS ON WORKING.

Oh, my! This is so *exciting!!*

SHE LANDS IN AN AVANT-GARDE BOOKSTORE IN PARIS.

ONE THING LEADS TO ANOTHER, AND PEGGY DISCOVERS THE MODERN ART GALLERIES. (SHE WOULD TURN THE PAINTINGS EVERY WHICH WAY TO FIGURE OUT WHICH POSITION IS RIGHT.)

SHE MEETS ALL THE ARTISTS AND WRITERS OF THE DAY: PICASSO, MAN RAY, DUCHAMP... AS WELL AS LAURENCE VAIL, WITH WHOM SHE FALLS IN LOVE.

Can... can I help you?

SHE IS FASCINATED BY THE EROTIC FRESCOES OF POMPEII. BUT ALL THE MEN IN HER SOCIAL CIRCLE FIND HER TOO RESPECTABLE TO SLEEP WITH.

Come now, Peggy! You're a *lady*.

IN THE END, LAURENCE VAIL IS THE ONE TO QUENCH HER CURIOSITY (AND EVEN MARRY HER).

Peggy is too attached to her name, so she becomes Mrs. Guggenheim-Vail.

BUT SHE QUICKLY GROWS BORED WITH MARRIAGE (EVEN THOUGH THEY TRAVEL CONSTANTLY AND ARE ALWAYS PARTYING WITH ARTISTS).

PEGGY IS CONVINCED THAT HER HUSBAND IS WAY TOO HANDSOME AND BRILLIANT FOR HER. PLUS, HE'S VIOLENT AND USES HER INSECURITIES AGAINST HER.

People only love you for your money!!

IN REALITY, PAINTERS LIKE PEGGY BECAUSE SHE SEEMS TO BE *IN LOVE* WITH ART.

I would easily travel three days to go see a painting.

AND WHILE SHE HERSELF DOESN'T MAKE ART, SHE ENCOURAGES OTHERS TO DO SO WHENEVER SHE CAN.

Seeing as you told me you'd love to take up photography...

TONS OF ARTISTS THEREFORE TRY TO EXTORT MONEY FROM HER, BUT PEGGY HAS VERY STRICT CRITERIA:

If I find it ugly, the answer's no.

SHE TRAVELS TO VENICE. SHE'S ENRAPTURED. THERE, FOR THE FIRST TIME, SHE DISCOVERS SHE LOVES BEING ALONE.

SHORTLY THEREAFTER, SHE AND LAURENCE HAVE TWO CHILDREN: SINBAD AND PEGEEN.

BUT THEN, IN RAPID SUCCESSION, HER BELOVED SISTER DIES IN CHILDBIRTH, THEN HER TWO NEPHEWS DIE UNDER SUSPICIOUS CIRCUMSTANCES. SHE IS DEVASTATED.

Her husband doesn't give a crap and lets her bawl her eyes out.

SHE LEAVES LAURENCE FOR LITERARY CRITIC JOHN HOLMS, WHOM SHE FINDS FASCINATING (AND WHO'S A BOOZEHOUND).

SHE GIVES AN ALLOWANCE TO LAURENCE AND HIS NEW WIFE (IN SECRET, SO HE WON'T FEEL HUMILIATED). THE CHILDREN ARE IN BOARDING SCHOOL IN SWITZERLAND. THEY'RE SPOILED ROTTEN AND HATE EVERYTHING.

JOHN DIES UNDER ANESTHESIA. (HE WAS DRUNK.) PEGGY MOURNS HIM ON THE SHOULDERS OF (LOTS OF) NEW LOVERS.

FOR SHE HAS *MANY* OF THEM. MOST ARE PAINTERS IN HER SOCIAL CIRCLE. THEY FASCINATE HER. ESPECIALLY THE REALLY GOOD-LOOKING ONES.

It sounds silly, but I feel less like the ugly duckling this way.

SHE LOVES ART AND ARTISTS. VISCERALLY. PHYSICALLY.

(BUT THIS DOESN'T MEAN SHE ISN'T DISCERNING.)

For instance, I *love* Dali's work, but I can't stand the man, you see.

AND THEN, HER MOTHER DIES, TOO. PEGGY FEELS COMPLETELY LOST. FOR THE LAST FIFTEEN YEARS, ALL SHE'S DONE IS PLAY THE ROLE OF WIFE.

I still don't know if I'm good at anything.

SHE DECIDES TO INVEST HER MONEY IN SOMETHING THAT, AT THE VERY LEAST, SHE KNOWS SHE LOVES: AN ART GALLERY, IN LONDON.

GUGGENHEIM JEUNE GALLERY

286

HER FRIEND MARCEL DUCHAMP HELPS HER UNDERSTAND SURREALISM, ABSTRACT ART, JEAN ARP'S BRONZES, AND COCTEAU'S DRAWINGS.

(HE ALSO INTRODUCES HER TO SAMUEL BECKETT, WHO IS JUST PEGGY'S TYPE.)

tortured
unfaithful
alcoholic

THEY'LL GO ON TO HAVE A TOXIC LOVE AFFAIR THAT LASTS FOR AGES.

FOR HER FIRST SHOW, SHE BRINGS IN MODERN WORKS FROM FRANCE. BUT CUSTOMS REFUSES TO ACCEPT THEM AS ART.

"Pieces of wood and metal"?!

FRAGI

SHE SHOWS THE WORKS OF FRIENDS OF FRIENDS: CALDER, TANGUY, KANDINSKY...

...AND STARTS THE HABIT OF ALWAYS BUYING A PIECE FROM THE ONE SHE LOVES THE MOST SO THEY WON'T FEEL BAD FOR NOT SELLING ANYTHING.

AND THAT IS HOW PEGGY STARTS BUILDING THE TWENTIETH CENTURY'S LARGEST COLLECTION OF MODERN ART.

IN NEW YORK, HER UNCLE SOLOMON R. GUGGENHEIM IS ALSO COLLECTING WORKS BY MASTERS FOR HIS FOUNDATION.

SHE OFFERS TO SELL HIM A FEW AVANT-GARDE PIECES.

SHE RECEIVES A RESPONSE WRITTEN BY HIS SECRETARY:

Dear Madam,

1. *This is not art.*

2. *We would rather die than buy anything from your gallery.*

All the best

P.S. Quit defiling the family name.

SHE ALSO EXHIBITS WORK BY CHILDREN, INCLUDING HER DAUGHTER PEGEEN, WHO LOVES TO PAINT.

Can I trade you for one of mine?

Picabia

IN FRANCE, SHE EVENTUALLY OPENS UP AN "ARTIST HOME," WHERE SHE HOUSES, FEEDS, AND GIVES SALARIES TO PAINTERS IN EXCHANGE FOR A PAINTING ONCE IN A WHILE.

René
Marcel
Max
Joan

SHE USUALLY SLEEPS WITH THEM, AS WELL.

(WHICH DOESN'T STOP HER FROM SUPPORTING THEIR WIVES.)

IN THESE DAYS, MODERN PAINTERS ARE STARVING ARTISTS. PEGGY DOES THE ROUNDS OF THE PARISIAN STUDIOS AND BUYS:

One painting a day!

LUCKY HER, SHE LOVES WHAT NOBODY ELSE WANTS IN THEIR HOMES: CUBISM.

BUT THEN THE NAZIS INVADE PARIS. PEGGY IS JEWISH, SHE HAS CHILDREN, AND YET SHE HAS ONLY *ONE* FEAR:

My babies! They'll destroy my babies!!!

SHE FINDS OUT THAT THE LOUVRE HAS A SECRET STORAGE PLACE TO PROTECT ITS PIECES.

SHE HOPES THEY WILL TAKE HER PAINTINGS TO KEEP THEM SAFE.

BUT THE MUSEUM REPLIES THAT HER COLLECTION "DOESN'T DESERVE TO BE SAVED."

We're talking Kandinsky, Picabia, Dali, Miró, and Magritte, among others!!

SHE PACKS UP HER KIDS, HER CATS, AND HER ARTWORK, AND HEADS BACK TO THE U.S.

No regrets!

NATURALLY, SHE ALSO MANAGES TO GET SCADS OF VISAS FOR HER SURREALISTS BEFORE SHE FLIES BACK.

André Breton

SHE EVEN TAKES A FEW BACK WITH HER (INCLUDING THEIR WIVES AND CHILDREN).

IN NEW YORK, SHE GETS THEM SITUATED, GIVES THEM MONTHLY ALLOWANCES, INTRODUCES THEM TO THE GUGGENHEIM NETWORK.

EVEN MAX ERNST (AND HIS LOVER). PEGGY IS CRAZY ABOUT HIM.

HE EVENTUALLY AGREES TO MARRY HER (FOR A GREEN CARD).

SHE'S VERY DISAPPOINTED: SHE HOPES TO BE HIS MUSE, BUT HE NEVER PAINTS HER, HE CHEATS ON HER INCESSANTLY, AND HE TELLS EVERYBODY HE'S ONLY IN IT FOR THE MONEY.

SHE CONSOLES HERSELF BY EXPANDING HER COLLECTION: MODERN ART HAS FLED EUROPE AND NOW BELONGS TO A HANDFUL OF MEN IN NEW YORK.

SHE SCOOPS UP EVERYTHING SHE LIKES, COMPULSIVELY.

IN 1942, SHE LAUNCHES A GALLERY IN MANHATTAN CALLED "ART OF THIS CENTURY." AT THE GRAND OPENING, SHE WEARS ONE EARRING DESIGNED FOR HER BY TANGUY AND ANOTHER BY CALDER.

It's to show my impartiality between surrealism and abstract art!

THE WALLS ARE CONCAVE. THE WORKS ARE HUNG FROM ROTATING WIRES SO PEOPLE CAN WALK AROUND THEM. PEGGY WANTS VISITORS TO HAVE AN UNUSUAL EXPERIENCE.

I love strange art because I'm strange.

BUT ERNST TELLS HER SHE'S BECOME BORING AND VULGAR EVER SINCE SHE OPENED HER GALLERY.

And it's not all about me anymore!

PEGGY DOES A GROUP SHOW FOR THIRTY-ONE WOMEN PAINTERS, INCLUDING THE BEAUTIFUL DOROTHEA TANNING.

MAX ERNST TAKES OFF WITH HER.

HER DAUGHTER IS VERY FRAGILE. SHE REGULARLY MOVES BACK HOME, DESPITE A COMPLICATED RELATIONSHIP WITH HER MOTHER.

BUT PEGEEN IS ALSO REMARKABLY ASTUTE.

All these artists are opportunistic, petty narcissists *who are using you*, Mom!

SO TRUE. PEGGY IS LIKE A MOTHER HEN TO THESE ARTISTS. SHE DISCOVERS THE WORK OF A CARPENTER IN HER UNCLE'S FUTURE MUSEUM.

What's your name?

Jackson Pollock.

SHE EXHIBITS HIM, MOTIVATES HIM, PAYS HIM, AND SUPPORTS HIM, EVEN THOUGH HE'S UTTERLY IMPOSSIBLE (AND THROWS UP AT HIS OWN OPENINGS).

He's an *artist*.

POLLOCK'S WORK STARTS TO SELL. REALLY SELL. PEGGY NO LONGER FEELS USEFUL IN THE U.S. SHE LONGS TO RETURN TO EUROPE AND START A NEW LIFE.

Do you know where you'll go?

Oh yes.

SHE PRESENTS HER ART COLLECTION AT THE VENICE BIENNALE. IT'S A HUGE HIT.

BUT ONCE THE SHOW IS OVER: WHAT TO DO WITH ALL THOSE PAINTINGS AND SCULPTURES?

SHE PURCHASES AN UNFINISHED PALAZZO ON THE GRAND CANAL AND MOVES IN WITH HER TREASURES.

her artwork

and her dogs

AT THE ENTRANCE TO HER PALACE, SHE DISPLAYS MARINI'S *ANGEL OF THE CITY*.

the detachable phallus is hidden when the nuns walk by

AND IN 1952, SHE FINALLY OPENS HER OWN MUSEUM, IN HER HOME.

THE PUBLIC WANTS TO SEE EVERYTHING, EVEN HER BEDROOM, SINCE CALDER DESIGNED HER HEADBOARD.

AFTER THAT, HER COLLECTION IS IN HIGH DEMAND: SHE LOANS IT OUT TO THE TATE IN LONDON, TO THE ORANGERIE IN PARIS...

EVEN HER UNCLE'S FOUNDATION WANTS IT...

Ha*!!* I bet he's turning over in his grave!

...FOR THE BRAND NEW SOLOMON R. GUGGENHEIM MUSEUM THAT HAS JUST OPENED ON FIFTH AVENUE IN MANHATTAN. PEGGY TRAVELS TO NEW YORK.

This is *awful!* It looks like a parking garage! The selection is lame! My uncle only cared about high-selling works! That was his only criteria!

290

GENERALLY SPEAKING, PEGGY IS SHOCKED BY THE DIRECTION THE MODERN ART MARKET IS TAKING: FINANCIAL INVESTMENTS, NOTHING MORE, AT SCANDALOUS PRICES, DEVOID OF TASTE OR PASSION.

I'd rather focus on African art.

IN 1965, PEGEEN COMMITS SUICIDE. FOR PEGGY, LIFE COMES TO A HALT. SHE DEDICATES A GALLERY IN HER MUSEUM TO HER DAUGHTER...

...WHERE SHE HANGS EVERYTHING PEGEEN HAD PAINTED SINCE SHE WAS TEN.

SHE EVENTUALLY AGREES TO DONATE HER COLLECTION TO HER LATE UNCLE'S FOUNDATION, PROVIDED THE PEGGY GUGGENHEIM MUSEUM REMAINS IN VENICE AND OPEN TO THE PUBLIC.

I want Venice to be a city of art.

And I want a *first name*.

SHE SPENDS A SIZABLE CHUNK OF HER FORTUNE WORKING TO SAVE VENICE FROM THE ENCROACHING SEA.

AND SHE USES THE REST TO GIVE CERTAIN ARTISTS ANNUITIES FOR LIFE.

TOWARD THE END OF HER LIFE, SHE TAKES TO HOSTING BIG DINNER PARTIES, WHERE THE FOOD, ACCORDING TO ALL HER FRIENDS, IS TERRIBLE.

I'm very proud of the life I've led. I just wish I were young, so I could have lovers, that's all.

SHE PASSES AWAY AT EIGHTY-ONE AND IS BURIED IN THE GARDEN OF HER MUSEUM-HOME, ALONG WITH HER FOURTEEN DOGS, AT THE FOOT OF A TREE PLANTED BY HER FRIEND YOKO ONO.

PEGGY GUGGENHEIM 1898-1979

CAPPUCINO
PEACOCK
TORO
FOGLIA
BABY
EMILY

FOREVER THE BLACK SHEEP, THE SELF-TAUGHT PEGGY HAD THE COURAGE TO FOLLOW HER OWN INTUITION IN AN UNFORGIVING, MALE-DOMINATED WORLD.

Artists sleep with everybody, and yet *I'm* the slut!

ALL HER FORTUNE, HER ENERGY, HER FLAIR, AND HER PASSION WERE DEVOTED TO KEEPING ART ALIVE AND MAKING IT ACCESSIBLE.

Her museum attracts millions of visitors every year.

NOBODY EVER LOVED PEGGY THE WAY SHE'D HOPED. BUT NOBODY EVER LOVED MODERN ART THE WAY SHE DID.

THIRTY MORE
REBEL LADIES WHO ROCKED THE WORLD

Phoolan Devi, *Bandit Queen of India*

Anne Bonny and Mary Read, *Pirates*

Isadora Duncan, *Dancer and Choreographer*

Marie Elizabeth Zakrzewska, *Rebel Midwife*

Zenobia, *Empress of the East*

Louise Yim, *Activist and Advocate for Korean Women*

Adeline and Augusta Van Buren, *Biker Sisters*

Valentina Tereshkova, *First Woman in Space*

Pamela Des Barres, *Muse of Rock 'n' Roll*

Tomoe Gozen, *Samurai*

Margaret Hamilton, *Computer Scientist of the Apollo Space Program*

Annie Edson Taylor, *First Person to Survive a Trip Over Niagara Falls in a Barrel*

Vaginal Davis, *Painter, Writer, and Musician*

Aisha Bakari Gombi, *Hunter of Antelopes and Boko Haram Militants*

Alice Guy-Blaché, *First Female Film Director*

Maya Angelou, *Poet*

Karen Horney, *Psychoanalyst who Challenged Freud*

Triêu Thi Trinh, *Elephant-Riding Warrior*

Hubertine Auclert, *Feminist and French Suffragette*

Marie Laveau, *Voodoo Queen of New Orleans*

Alexandra David-Néel, *Opera Singer, Explorer, Anarchist, Philosopher, and Spiritualist*

Tarpé Mills, *One of the First Female Artists in Superhero Comics*

Helen Thomas, *White House Correspondent from Kennedy to Obama*

Anne Sullivan, *Helen Keller's Teacher*

Imogen Cunningham, *Photographer*

Carmen Herrera, *Centenarian and Painter*

Margaret Sanger, *Nurse and Founder of Planned Parenthood*

Qiu Jin, *Saber-Fighting Journalist*

Simone Veil, *Auschwitz Survivor and Champion for the Legalization of Abortion*

Laskarina Bouboulina, *Admiral, Ship-Builder, and Harem Liberator*

1982–

PÉNÉLOPE IS BORN IN 1982 IN PARIS.

HER FAMILY IS FROM FRENCH BASQUE COUNTRY AND CORSICA, TWO AREAS IN FRANCE THAT ARE FAMOUS FOR THEIR CHEESE AND THEIR SEPARATIST MOVEMENTS.

My god!

What a grouch! Is she Corsican? Basque?

Both.

← (true story)

TO PROMOTE PEACE AND QUIET AT HOME, HER PARENTS STUFF HER HANDS WITH CRAYONS WHEN SHE'S TWO.

Pénélope!!!

SHE DECLARES THAT WHEN SHE GROWS UP, SHE'LL SET UP SHOP AND SELL HER DRAWINGS ON THE STREET.

(And also become queen of America.)

WITH HER BIG SISTER CLÉMENTINE, SHE SPENDS HER SPARE TIME CREATING FAN FICTION COMICS OF THEIR IDOLS: **QUEEN.**

I think I prefer his "I Want to Break Free" mustache.

PÉNÉLOPE HATES SCHOOL AND SEES THESE YEARS AS A LONG TUNNEL TOWARD FREEDOM.

Bagieu! Bring that over to me!

ALL SHE WANTS TO DO IS LISTEN TO ROCK MUSIC, PLAY HER SUPER NINTENDO, AND DRAW ILLUSTRATIONS FOR *MAGIC: THE GATHERING.*

But I guess I can't make a living doing that.

HER MOM PROMISES THAT WHEN SHE'S DOING THE THING SHE LOVES, TIME WILL FLY.

So do exactly what you want with your life, understand?

FOLLOWING THIS GREAT ADVICE, AFTER GRADUATING FROM HIGH SCHOOL SHE ENTERS AN ART COLLEGE IN PARIS CALLED ENSAD.

People like me!!

AND INDEED, TIME FLIES.

SHE GETS HER DEGREE AND STARTS TO WORK AS AN EDITORIAL AND COMMERCIAL ILLUSTRATOR.

I'm getting *paid* to *stay home* and *draw*??

Is this a trap?

A MAGAZINE INVITES HER TO CREATE A WEEKLY COMIC STRIP. THAT'S NEW AND SCARY FOR PÉNÉLOPE, AND HER BRAIN IS SCREAMING AT HER TO REFUSE (AT FIRST).

Come on! It's not harder than drawing Freddie Mercury! You can do it!

THE COMIC STRIPS ARE THEN COLLECTED INTO A BOOK THAT IS QUITE SUCCESSFUL. SO SHE MAKES ANOTHER BOOK, AND ANOTHER, AND MANY MORE.

I guess you could say selling my drawings on the street is my job now.

AT THE AGE OF THIRTY-TWO, SHE FINALLY DECIDES TO LIVE SOME PLACE OTHER THAN GOOD OLD PARIS.

I know I can never be queen of America, but oh well.

WICKED

And she still can't draw cars!

IN NEW YORK CITY SHE HAS AN IDEA: EVERY WEEK, SHE'LL TELL THE STORY OF A WOMAN WHO DID EXACTLY WHAT SHE WANTED WITH HER LIFE.

Katia Krafft

AND ALL THOSE STORIES LED TO THE BOOK YOU'RE READING RIGHT NOW.

Yes, *you.*

BRAZEN IS TRANSLATED IN ABOUT TEN LANGUAGES, AND PÉNÉLOPE STILL SPENDS HER DAYS DRAWING AND LISTENING TO ROCK MUSIC.

ALSO AVAILABLE FROM PÉNÉLOPE BAGIEU

"Pénélope Bagieu has mastered a magic trick, and it is this: Somehow, even as she suspends our disbelief, she can turn paper into flesh. And ink becomes lifeblood . . . her characters not only breathe and pulsate with vivid life. They also seem entirely, organically authentic in their own skin."
—*The Washington Post*

"Wonderful . . . her cartooning style is a sheer delight."
—*Mental Floss*

"Exuberance and sadness coexist in her drawing style, as they coexist in the character of Cass Elliot— whose every moment of joy and perseverance seems to overlay deep loneliness and vulnerability."
—*The New York Times*

"Bagieu's drawings are superlative: soft pencil lines that convey detail without constraining her figures and that animate the characters' exuberant facial expressions."
—*The Paris Review*

1 3 5 7 9 10 8 6 4 2

Ebury Press, an imprint of Ebury Publishing,
20 Vauxhall Bridge Road, London, SW1V 2SA

Ebury Press is part of the Penguin Random House group of companies whose
addresses can be found at global.penguinrandomhouse.com

Penguin
Random House
UK

English translation by Montana Kane
English translation Copyright © Pénélope Bagieu 2018

Pénélope Bagieu has asserted her right to be identified as the author of this Work
in accordance with the Copyright, Designs and Patents Act 1988

First published by Ebury Press in 2018

Originally published in French by Gallimard in 2016 as Culottées: Des femmes
qui ne font que cequ'elles veulent, tome I and in 2017 as Culottées: Des femmes
qui ne font que ce qu'elles veulent, tome II

Some of the pages in this book were previously published on the author's blog
"Culottées" hosted by the website of the French daily newspaper Le Monde, lemonde.fr

French text and illustrations copyright © 2016, 2017 by Gallimard

www.penguin.co.uk

A CIP catalogue record for this book is available from the British Library

Design: Chris Dickey and Danielle Ceccolini
Lionel Text Diesel © Font Diner www.fontdiner.com

Special thanks to Farah Rishi and Muslim Squad

ISBN: 978-1-78503-903-4

Printed and bound in Italy by L.E.G.O. S.p.A

Penguin Random House is committed to a sustainable future for
our business, our readers and our planet. This book is made from
Forest Stewardship Council® certified paper

MIX
Paper from
responsible sources
FSC® C018179
FSC
www.fsc.org